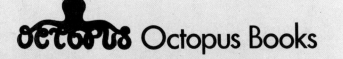 Octopus Books

The Movie Treasury

GANGSTER MOVIES

The Movie Treasury

GANGSTER MOVIES

Gangsters,
Hoodlums and
Tough Guys of the
Screen

HARRY HOSSENT

CONTENTS

NOTE. The dates of films given throughout this book are approximate. This is because of varying lengths of production-period, the intervals between production and distribution and differing dates of distribution in various territories. In most cases the date given is the year of principal production.

MOVIES are fun. This book is intended to show that the gangster movie is fun. All too often, books about the film tend to look on the making of a movie as though a great work of art had been conceived in the minds of the producer and director at the moment when the cameras started turning. This is unlikely. What is more likely is that the producer said: "Hey! We've got a good story here!" and the director said: "I like that!" and the picture went into production. In after years, when careful critics assessed the film, the work of art was born, but at the time it was being made, nobody had any other ideas but to turn an honest pound, dollar or yen. I am reminded of a colour film which broke into black and white at certain points and, when it was screened, the critics said: "That's wonderful . . . the director used black and white in those sequences to make a particular point." Unfortunately, the director later admitted: "I used black and white because we were running out of money and the only stock I could afford was black and white."

So don't look at the gangster movies too deeply. They were produced to make a profit at a time when gangster movies made a profit. And all films about criminal violence since then have been made with this same end in view. To paraphrase something which Sam Goldwyn is reputed to have said: "If you want to deliver a message, call Western Union."

GANGSTERS, HOODLUMS AND TOUGH GUYS

THE WEATHER in Chicago that spring afternoon of 1920 was sultry, foreshadowing the heat of summer. At Colosimo's Restaurant on 2126 South Wabash Avenue, the important business of selecting the evening's dinner menu was just beginning. "Big Jim" Colosimo, owner of the restaurant, stepped out of his office for a moment to walk through the two dining rooms into the small vestibule which gave on to the street. The time was 4.25.

A moment later two shots were heard. Frank Camilla, "Big Jim's" secretary, dashed through the restaurant to see what had happened. He found "Big Jim" lying face downwards on the tiled floor of the vestibule, a bullet wound behind his right ear. A second bullet had buried itself in the wall.

"Big Jim" Colosimo, restaurant-owner, brothel-keeper and opium-runner, was dead.

That is not a scene from a Hollywood gangster film. "Big Jim" Colosimo – sometimes he was known as "Diamond Jim" because of his fondness for the gems – was murdered on 11 May 1920, less than a year after Prohibition came to the United States of America.

It was, however, a scene which has been immortalized in scores of movies. The middle-aged big-shot, apparently secure in his position of criminal power. The moment of relaxation, a greeting, perhaps, for an old friend. Close shot of the second man's face as he drops his mask of friendship. Close shot of Colosimo as he realizes – too late – what is about to happen. Mid-shot of second man as he draws a gun. "This is for you, Jim." Two-shot of Colosimo and killer as the shots are fired and "Big Jim" falls to the tiled floor.

By now, that type of scene almost parodies itself. Only the most unsuspecting of filmgoers would fail to recognize that "Big Jim" was for it, the moment he stepped into the vestibule. We have all read the script and we know the action.

Loosely, this kind of movie is called a gangster film. It is as good a description as any, though the film of criminal violence is not always about gang-sters, but often about petty crooks, thieves, con-men, hoodlums and mobsters of all kinds. In these cynical 'Seventies, the toughest guy of all is just as likely to be a policeman, one who is himself only just inside the law. Anthony Quinn's New York police captain in *Across 110th Street* ruthlessly pursues killers through the entire film; two-thirds of the way into the plot, however, we learn that he is taking a regular bribe from a black gang-boss.

Think of Clint Eastwood in *Dirty Harry*. He is a plain-clothes policeman who is as ready to shoot down a criminal as arrest him. "Uh-huh," he says, as he stands with drawn revolver over a bank-robber lying on the sidewalk. "I know what you're thinkin': 'Did he fire six shots or only five?' Well, to tell you truth in all this excitement I've kinda lost track myself. But bein' this is a forty-four Magnum, the most powerful hand-gun in the world, and would blow your head clean off . . . you've got to ask yourself one question: 'Do I feel lucky?' Well, do you, punk?"

Though the violence is under cover and only expressed through the grossness of the big .44 in Eastwood's fist, that is about as violent a little scene as one is likely to see on the screen.

If violence is basic to crime movies, so is romance – if one defines romance as the experience of being the other man, in the other place, at the other time. At some time or another, most of us have wanted to be tough cops or snarling gunmen or laconic private detectives . . . just so long as we did not have to face the realities that accompany those roles. Fantasy, if you like. But it explains the continued popularity of the thriller, from Bulldog Drummond to James Bond. It is the fast-cars-in-the-night fantasy somewhere in the rain-drenched, dimly-lit sidewalks of our minds.

Those shots on South Wabash Avenue in 1920 could, in film terms, be likened to the *thwack* of the slate for Scene One, Take One of "*The Violent Screen*."

LEFT *". . . this is a forty-four Magnum, the most powerful hand-gun in the world . . ." Clint Eastwood standing over Andy Robinson in* Dirty Harry *(WB/Malpaso 1971)*

Booze Began It

Gangsters, hoodlums and tough guys . . . scores of them have been portrayed on the screen. They may have been disguised under names invented by the screenwriters, but all of them have been based – if sometimes rather broadly – on flesh-and-blood criminals. And all of them, up there in black-and-white or Technicolor, owe their screen existences to three events in American history: the years of the Depression, the development of the talking picture, and the rise of Al Capone.

Al Capone built an empire of crime the like of which has never since been controlled by one man alone. He was undoubtedly a man who lived out of his time; several hundred years before, he would have been a robber baron whose descendants would today be respectable members of some European aristocracy. But he happened to be born in 1895, not 1195; and his family took him from Italy to America as a baby.

ABOVE LEFT *In the days before he turned cop; . . . or was he a policeman put into a cell with Roger Touhy? A young Anthony Quinn (left) with Preston Foster (playing Roger Touhy) in* The Last Gangster *(20th Century-Fox 1945)*

BELOW LEFT *Booze began it. Didn't it just? When the Feds moved in the booze barrels were smashed and beer ran freely.* The Scarface Mob *(Desilu 1959)*

ABOVE *Clint Eastwood in a scene from* Magnum Force *(Malpaso 1973)*

"I'm a public benefactor," "Big Al" once remarked. "They call Capone a bootlegger. Yeah – it's bootleg while it's on the trucks, but when your host at the club, in the locker room or on the Gold Coast hands it to you on a silver platter, it's hospitality . . . Some call it bootlegging. Some call it racketeering. I call it a business."

Conveniently, he forgot to mention that, like other mobsters of the period, he was also involved in illegal bookmaking, prostitution, various protection rackets . . . and wholesale murder on the side. But robber barons also slew without mercy, and today we regard their murderous activities as acts of war against their enemies. The difference between Al Capone and the Black Knight is only one of time.

In 1920, "Big Jim" Colosimo was ready to settle down. After years of running brothels and dope around Chicago's notorious Levee – where the Chicago Vice Commission put the 1910 gross takings from prostitution alone at $60,000,000 – he had fallen in love with a beautiful brunette who had aspirations to become an opera singer. Dale Winter, 19, was singing in the South Park Avenue Methodist Church when she became the star attraction of the Colosimo Restaurant floor show. In fact, she continued to sing for the church until a scandalized congregation discovered where she also entertained by night . . . and promptly said: "Go!"

A more unlikely girl-friend for a gangster it would be impossible to find. Not only was Dale

Winter a talented soprano, she was also a demure young woman of impeccable taste who brought elegance and refinement to the restaurant. There is an echo of her story in *On Wings Of Song* (American title: *Love Me Forever*), an early Grace Moore film in which Leo Carrillo, as a gangster-cum-restaurateur, loving Miss Moore from afar, hires the singer to "give a touch of class to the joint." The publicity blurb for this film is particularly choice: "The story of a girl with a God-given voice who becomes the protégé of a wealthy gambler. This man, moulded by adversity and life's bitter blows, worships fine music . . . he loves and dies for an ideal."

Miss Winter, however, did make the mistake of falling in love with Colosimo and – after his divorce – marrying him. The marriage lasted less than a month and ended with Colosimo's murder on 11 May 1920.

Earlier, Colosimo had been threatened by extortionists, and to protect his life he had imported his nephew, Johnny Torrio, from the infamous Five Points Gang of New York. Torrio, quiet, unobtrusive, working as "Big Jim's" business manager from ten until six, had already dealt effectively with the threats. Later, he brought two men from the Five Points Gang to Chicago to "put the finger" on anyone who threatened "Big Jim". One of them was Frankie Yale. The other was Alphonse Capone, who arrived under the alias he used on many occasions: Al Brown. Vincenzo Cosmano, who demanded $10,000 from Colosimo, took a shotgun blast for his pains and though he survived it, decided to leave town.

By the time Colosimo fell in love with his songbird, the whisper had gone around Chicago: "Big Jim's slipping." He no longer controlled his vice district with an iron hand. Matters of business were left to Torrio who could see that his uncle's power was in decline.

To this day it has never been officially established who fingered "Big Jim". Johnny Torrio, seeing the vast profits which could be made from the manufacture and sale of illegal liquor as a result of the new Prohibition law, had long been urging him to get into this new racket. But Colosimo did not want to know. He was wealthy; living up to his name as "Diamond Jim", he wore diamond rings on several fingers, had his tiepin, shirt-cuffs and waistcoat studded with diamonds, and even carried with

PREVIOUS PAGES *Edward G. Robinson with Peter Falk and Robert Foulk in* Robin and the 7 Hoods *(P-C 1964)*
LEFT *John Wayne walking away from a wrecked car in* McQ *(Batjac/Levy-Gardener 1974)*
ABOVE *Marrying singer Dale Winter led indirectly to "Big Jim" Colosimo's death*

him little chamois bags of diamonds which, in idle moments, he would empty on his desk and fondle lovingly. He was also growing respectable; the association with Dale Winter had led to his hiring a tutor to teach him to speak correctly, and he was cultivating the friendship of "society" while neglecting his former underworld companions.

It was time for Colosimo to go. Probably the fatal shots were fired by Frankie Yale, who had again fortuitously appeared in Chicago a week before the murder. Almost certainly they were inspired by Johnny Torrio, who lost no time in stepping into his uncle's shoes.

He also upgraded Al Brown from brothel pimp and minor bodyguard to make him a "partner" in the crime kingdom left by Colosimo. The way was clear for the great gang battles of the 1920's against opposition like the Dion O'Banion gang on the North Side, the Spike O'Donnell gang on the South, and Terry Druggan and Frank Lake to the West.

Eventually the Torrio-Capone partnership faded. Johnny Torrio, after a running car- and gun-battle with "Little Hymie" Weiss, George "Bugs" Moran and Schemer Drucci, decided to leave town. He fled to New York and joined up with the local gang boss, "Dutch" Schultz. Al Capone became the "Big Fellow" in Chicago.

Many of the early gangster films were based, somewhat loosely, on the exploits of these notorious thugs. Between 1930 and 1932 about 60 gangster movies were made in Hollywood. *Little Caesar* began the cycle, to be followed by *Public Enemy* and *Scarface*. These are the three most important gangster films of all time because they set the pattern for the true gangster movie, just as John Huston's version of *The Maltese Falcon* was the mould for all private eye pictures, and John Ford's *Stagecoach* stylized the screen Western.

Little Caesar, a Warner Brothers-First National production directed by Mervyn Le Roy, was made in 1930 and featured Edward G. Robinson and

"Al Capone built an empire of crime the like of which has never since been controlled by one man alone." Nevertheless, he once remarked that he was a public benefactor. The composite picture (above) *shows Capone with Rod Steiger who played him in* Al Capone *(Burrows-Ackerman-Allied Artists 1958). Check the real Capone against the picture* (right) *showing him as he was in 1929*

ABOVE *Leo Carrillo played a vague sort of "Big Jim" Colosimo in* On Wings of Song *(Columbia 1935)*
BELOW *Shooting came naturally to the Capone gang, as this scene from* The St. Valentine's Day Massacre *(Los Altos/20th Century-Fox 1967) shows*

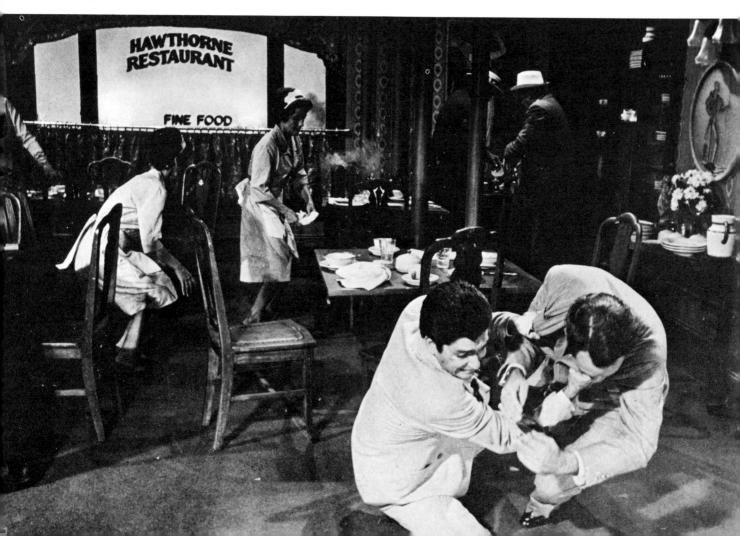

Douglas Fairbanks, Jr. It was adapted by William Riley Burnett from his own novel of the same name.

From then on, until the early gangster cycle had run its course, Warners seemed to have a monopoly on the rackets. The company followed *Little Caesar* with *Public Enemy*, directed by William Wellman, in 1931. It made famous the names of Robinson, Cagney and Bogart as hard-bitten, snarling gang chiefs or gunmen. It also created what amounted to a repertory company of featured players in the black-and-white world of mobsters: actors like Allen Jenkins, Frank McHugh, Glenda Farrell, James Gleason, Pat O'Brien, Joan Blondell, Mae Clarke, Eduardo Cianelli and many others became familiar faces among the tommy-guns and Chevrolets of the city streets.

The novel from which *Little Caesar* was adapted tells the story of Rico, a small-time crook who rises to become a big shot in Chicago – though not the "Big Fellow" himself. It is told in W. R. Burnett's typically laconic, understated style and the adaptation, especially tailored for the image of a dapper, snarling Edward G. – an image completely unlike the actor's real character, but one which fostered scores of imitations and followed Robinson throughout his entire career – does not bear too much resemblance to the book.

Here is one complete chapter – yes, one chapter! – from *Little Caesar* which describes Rico perfectly:

CHAPTER VI

Rico was standing in front of his mirror, combing his hair with a little ivory pocket-comb. Rico was vain of his hair. It was black and lustrous, combed straight back from his low forehead and arranged in three symmetrical waves.

Rico was a simple man. He loved but three things: himself, his hair and his gun. He took excellent care of all three.

This was a new style of writing, owing something to Hemingway and much to American newspaper police reporting and the pulp magazines of the period. It was good screenwriting, too. Men like Ben Hecht, Mark Hellinger and Dashiel Hammett were highly experienced in this form; later, Raymond Chandler perfected the technique in such classics as *The Big Sleep* and *Lady In The Lake*; later still, Ross Macdonald updated it to the '60's with books like *The Moving Target*.

But Edward G. brought the characters to life on the screen. At the moment when, as Rico in *Little Caesar*, he snarled: "All right, you guys – I'm boss here – see?" the gangster film was born.

It was not to last, of course, and in fact those early gangster movies, in which the action was seen from the standpoint of the criminal himself, raced across the screen for a brief two or three years. The gangster met his just deserts in the last reel, true, but during the rest of the picture he was the central figure. The Good Guys triumphed in the end, but it always seemed as though this was something of an afterthought. For most of the film, the Good Guys – in the shape of police and newspaper reporters – tended to have their faces rubbed in the mud. The Hays Office issued a warning. A boycott of gangster films was threatened by the American Legion and similar influential U.S. organisations. By 1933, the gangster film had suffered a sea-change and the stories were told through the viewpoints of the Good Guys, fighting the evil of mobsterism.

In 40 years, the wheel has turned a full cycle. Consider the character played by Lee Marvin in *Prime Cut*. He is a "hit man", a torpedo who can be hired by the new breed of businessman-gangster. Pressured into a job against his will, he is sent to Kansas City to enforce his employer's demands for payment from another gangster-type. From then on, a trail of murder, mayhem and killing makes the screen run red. If the baddies all come to sticky ends – so does at least one innocent person, whom Marvin involves – as in the case of the truck-driver whose vehicle he hijacks.

It is a tremendously exciting film, if one disregards its moral values. At the end Marvin, the paid killer who keeps the weapons of his trade in velvet-lined cases, has destroyed all the other villains . . . yet walks off into the sunset without a hint of retribution. Certainly, it is a film which would never have passed the censor in the '30's – when crime was not allowed to pay – on the screen at any rate.

Nevertheless, the film stars who played these gangsters – Robinson, Cagney and Bogart – were popular heroes in America at a time when people badly needed heroes – the Depression years. The politicians, they felt, had deceived them; they had lost faith in bankers and businessmen. But film stars lived in a style which seemed miraculously untouched by breadlines and bank crashes. They were safe – or appeared to be safe – from the unemployment that beset Americans in all walks of life . . . and, as the Depression became worldwide, film-goers everywhere.

Gangsters, too, could be heroes. They were the ultimate exponents of free enterprise . . . and they

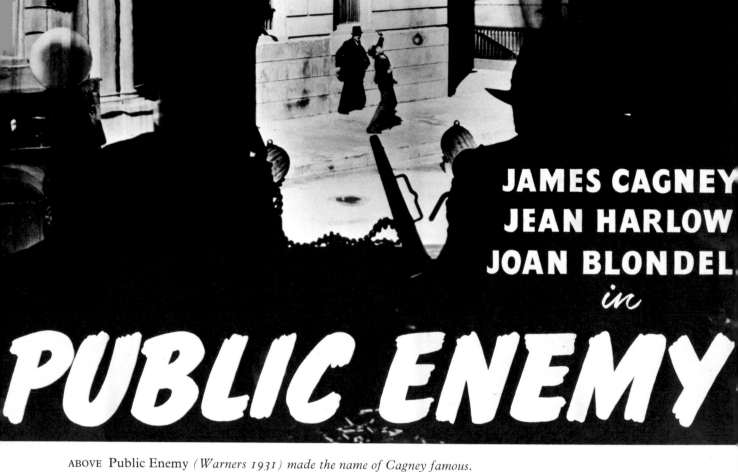

JAMES CAGNEY
JEAN HARLOW
JOAN BLONDEL
in

PUBLIC ENEMY

ABOVE Public Enemy *(Warners 1931) made the name of Cagney famous.*
It also billed Jean Harlow, who was soon to make her fame alone
BELOW *Cagney's portrayals of gangsters always had an element of*
"mommism" in them. This is noticeable in Public Enemy *(Warners 1931)*
where Mom (right) was played by Beryl Mercer

were successful. Criminal, perhaps . . . but wasn't everyone crooked those days? The "Big Fellow" himself had commented: "They say I violate the prohibition law. Who doesn't?" They were exciting, and ordinary people badly needed exciting personalities to take their minds off poverty and the dole.

But if the real gangster film was bred in the Depression, it was foreshadowed in 1927 by Josef von Sternberg's silent film, *Underworld,* the first film of violence to tell a mobster's story from a mobster's viewpoint. Though rarely shown today, *Underworld* is notable for the performance of George Bancroft, a successful New York stage actor who went to Hollywood in 1922. He played "Bull" Weed, a great laughing giant of a man who roars through the film like a whirlwind. He robs banks, battles with the police and, in the end, gives himself up after believing for a time that his friends and associates have betrayed him.

Sternberg himself, in his book "Fun In A Chinese Laundry", has much to say about *Underworld.* "I completed the film in four weeks," he wrote. "The author of the original idea, Mr. Hecht, was first heard from. His telegram said: 'You poor ham take my name off the film.'"

Nevertheless, the film was a roaring success. According to von Sternberg, it opened in New York at ten a.m. to avoid being reviewed by the Press. "Three hours later," he wrote, "no one knows why or how, Times Square was blocked by a huge crowd seeking to gain admission to the theatre, a crowd that stayed there and forced the theatre to stay open all night and remain open all night for the balance of the long run, thus inaugurating the era of gangster films and exhibitions of films around the clock."

Playing opposite George Bancroft was Evelyn Brent, as "Feathers" – probably the first of the gangster girls on screen. In the film she got her name because of the feathered dresses she wore; according to von Sternberg, he also had feathers sewn into her underwear to complete the illusion.

Based on a story by Ben Hecht, with screenplay by Robert N. Lee, the film is, however, very much a stylized conception of hoodlums, made with all the cinematic poetry of which von Sternberg was capable. It owes more to the Germanic overtones of *Dr Mabuse* than it does to the *Chicago Tribune.* Furthermore, "Bull" Weed is not a gangster in the Capone pattern; he robs banks instead of existing on an empire of booze and vice. The characters seem to live in a dream world which had little to do with the city streets of the 1920's. They are not

documented gangsters lifted from the news-pages and enlarged upon, but more figures in a grand tragedy. For that one must look to von Sternberg.

Though considered to be the first gangster picture, *Underworld* was not followed by a wave of similar films. *Scarface* and the rest awaited the arrival of "talkies".

Sound on picture opened the way for a kind of action which had never before been possible. A gun shot in the silent days was normally signalled by the crack of a trap-drum from the orchestra pit – if the pianist was quick off the mark. The roar of Chevrolets and Buicks through city streets was accompanied by "chase" music.

It did not happen immediately, of course, because the early talking equipment was not flexible enough to permit action films to be made without great difficulty. Three years had to pass while Hollywood assimilated the idea of the talking picture and learned what to do with it. The "blimped" camera had to be invented; the sound "boom" had to be introduced. Playback required to be developed and an improvement had to be made in back-projection systems to get the talking picture out of the drawing-room and into wider locations. Even then, action sequences were shot inside the studio for many years.

Scarface, Shame of a Nation – to give the film its full title – is the film of the 1930's which is most often brought up in discussions on the gangster movie. Produced for United Artists in 1931 by Howard Hughes, in conjunction with Howard Hawks, it was directed by Hawks from a screenplay by Ben Hecht.

There are probably more legends about *Scarface* than about any other gangs and guns picture. One of them is that Al Capone, hearing of plans to make the film, demanded that the script be submitted to him for approval. Ben Hecht has said that one night two hoodlum-types called on him with a copy of the script – which they had somehow obtained – and asked if it really was about Al. He persuaded them it had nothing to do with the "Big Fellow" and, apparently satisfied, they went their way. Another story is that the producers offered Capone $200,000 to appear in the film . . . and if that little tale does not suggest a studio publicity man's dream, nothing ever will.

According to Hawks, he directed *Scarface* with the idea of telling the story of the Capone family as if they were the Borgias living in Chicago in the '20's. This may well be true. At the time, however, there was much publicity to suggest that *Scarface* was the Capone story – which it certainly wasn't.

ABOVE Scarface *(United Artists 1932) is a film "devised to exploit the Chicago of its day"*
BELOW Public Enemy *created the Cagney image, but he went on to perfect it, in the two-gun tough style, as in this shot from* Angels with Dirty Faces *(WB 1938)*
BELOW RIGHT *"You swine . . ." "No . . . not this".* Scarface *(United Artists 1932) was a good movie although you wouldn't think so from the stills*

It was a very good, exciting gangster film, and it stands up well when viewed today, more than 40 years on. Compared with present-day underplaying, the acting has a broadness which at times verges almost on the laughable. Try to watch it as one would watch a modern film, and the great dramatic moments fail to come across – particularly in television revivals, where on the small screen the film is not seen to best advantage. This is not the fault of the film; over nearly half a century, screen acting has changed out of all recognition.

Paul Muni gave a great performance as Tony Camonte, the scarred gang-leader, but it bears little resemblance to Capone as he really was. Camonte is tough, ruthless, a handy man with a gun and – at the end – a figure hysterically afraid of death as he battles it out with police from his steel-shuttered fortress. Capone was certainly tough and ruthless, but he tried to avoid gunplay himself and employed others to do his dirty work. He was not cowardly, and he did not die in battle. The nickname of "Scarface" was one applied to him only in newspapers and magazines: to his friends and associates, he was always "Al", and if anyone had addressed him as "Scarface" the famous Capone fury would immediately have been aroused. It was the same with other mobsters. "Little Hymie" Weiss, "Schemer" Drucci, "Greasy Thumb" Jack Guzik, "Bugs" Moran . . . these were names invented by the crime writers of the Chicago tabloids.

Scarface should be seen and remembered as a film devised to exploit the Chicago of its day – and it must be remembered that Chicago gang wars made front-page banner headlines all over the world. It is the story of a battle for power between two gangster figures: Tony Camonte and Gaffney, played by Boris Karloff. A secondary plot hinges on Camonte's strength of feeling for his sister, Cesca (Ann Dvorak), and the romance between Cesca and Camonte's henchman, Guino Rinaldo (George Raft).

Eventually Camonte kills Rinaldo in the belief that he has violated Cesca – though the pair are actually married. This is the famous scene in which Rinaldo, whose trademark throughout the picture is his constant flipping and catching of a gold coin, drops out of picture as he dies . . . and the coin this time falls to the floor.

Gaffney, the rival gang-leader, is sometimes likened to Edward "Spike" O'Donnell, with whom Capone fought a war for control of the Chicago South Side. In the film, however, the Gaffney character is totally unlike the real Spike, who was a rough-and-ready criminal of Irish descent with a tendency towards practical jokes. He and his three brothers, Steve, Walter and Tommy, did just about everything in their time, from bank robberies to strike-breaking, with a little pickpocketing on the side. "Spike" was a devout Catholic who attended services regularly . . . yet his most-quoted remark is: "When arguments fail – use a black-jack."

Public Enemy, produced by Darryl F. Zanuck and directed by William Wellman, brought two things to the screen: the cocky, fast-talking, unscrupulous gangster characterization by James Cagney which was to follow him throughout his entire screen career . . . and the grapefruit scene. Even today, comedians have only to bounce into the Cagney pose and snarl: "Yuh dirty rats!" to evoke a wave of nostalgic laughter from older audiences.

Though Public Enemy created the Cagney image, he had already appeared in two other

gangster films for Warners, as a murderer prepared
to let someone else pay for his crime in *Sinner's
Holiday*, and as a double-crossing hoodlum in
Doorway to Hell. *Public Enemy*, however, was a
bigger-budget production, directed by William
Wellman, and it contained all the elements of
success: Rotha and Griffith, in their book, *The
Film Till Now*, described the gangsters as being
"detailed with a realism new to the screen. In
danger more from rival gangsters than from the
police, they moved uneasily from apartment to
apartment, their surroundings at once luxurious
and sordid, their women women and nothing
more."

It is the story of two brothers who become
Chicago booze barons in the 1920's. One was
Edward Woods, the other Cagney; at the start of
shooting, what is now the Cagney part was played
by Woods, and vice versa. Within three days it was
seen that the roles would be better reversed.
Wellman persuaded the two actors to change parts,
and Cagney began to make screen history.

It is sometimes claimed that the story of *Public
Enemy* is based on that of "Little Hymie" Weiss,
leader of the North Side Chicago gang after the
murder of Dion O'Banion by the Capones in 1924.
What is more likely is that the Cagney characterization is based on "Little Hymie"; the plot itself is
pure fiction.

A Chicago newspaperman, writing about Weiss
in 1930, said: "In many respects this sardonic Pole
was Gangland's most amazing personality and,
had he lived, he would surely have become the Big
Fellow. Weiss was a man of tremendous courage

despite his slight stature. He was capable of un-
believable rages, and long periods of moody
silence . . . 'Little Hymie', who had a premonition
of an early death, once said that although he didn't
expect to live long, he did expect to live long
enough."

When Cagney, in his striped pyjamas, sat
opposite Mae Clarke at breakfast and decided he
had had enough of this boring broad, he wasted no
time. He picked up half a grapefruit and planted it
full into Miss Clarke's face. It was a piece of
screen action which has lasted down the years as
the ultimate in violence from the gangster to his
moll.

Of course, it isn't – it just seems that way.
Since then girls have been slapped, kicked,
beaten up, run over, shot, stabbed and raped, all
in the tradition of mobster violence.

But at the time this scene was daring, and the
more daring because it was totally unexpected.
"When I first saw *Public Enemy*," wrote Donovan
Pedelty, Hollywood correspondent of the 1930's,
"the preview audience just gasped at this scene."

We remember Mae Clarke in *Public Enemy*, yet
forget that Jean Harlow was in it, too. There may
have been good reason. The *New York Times*,
reviewing the film in 1931, commented: "The
acting throughout is interesting, with the exception
of Jean Harlow."

We also remember the final scene. Cagney, cut to
pieces by bullets, is carried to the door of his
mother's apartment by the hoods who have shot
him. They press the door-bell. As the door is
opened, he falls lifeless into the hall.

THE CHICAGO PIANO

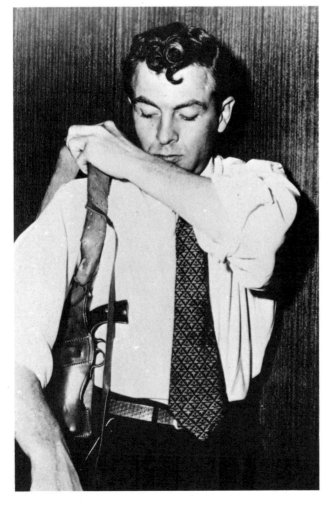

THE SYMBOL of the gangster, and of films about him, is the "Chicago piano".

It's also called a "typewriter" and a "chopper" and it is, in fact, the Model 21A Thompson sub-machine gun, usually fitted with a 50-cartridge drum magazine. Named after Brigadier General John T. Thompson, U.S. Director of Arsenals during World War I – and one of the inventors of the gun – it had a significant advantage in the Roaring 'Twenties: while most American cities had outlawed ownership of small hand-guns, they had somehow forgotten about the tommy-gun and, in fact, anyone could buy a tommy quite openly.

It was also light enough – weighing in at eight and a half pounds – to be easily portable; it could fire at the rate of a thousand .45 calibre cartridges a minute; and at close range could penetrate quarter inch steel armour plate. You didn't get shot by a "Chicago piano": you got cut in two.

Modern versions of the Thompson use .45 ammunition and a 20 or 30-round detachable magazine. Despite all those long bursts of tommy-gun fire from drum magazine "choppers" which

ABOVE LEFT *"You didn't get shot by a 'Chicago piano', you got cut in two".*
A symphony on seven pianos from Baby Face Nelson *(Fryman-Zimbalist 1957)*
LEFT *Putting on the heater; a scene from* I, The Jury *(Parklane 1953)*
ABOVE *Mickey Rooney demonstrating the "Chicago piano" in another scene from* Baby Face Nelson *(Fryman-Zimbalist 1957)*

can still be seen in TV re-runs of old gangster films, it has to be admitted that the drum magazine was not exceptionally efficient. It tended to jam too often.

These days the machine-pistol has largely superseded the original Thompson. Favourite – particularly among revolutionaries – is the Czech-built AK47, a gas-operated assault rifle which fires either single shots or, switched to automatic, will use up a 30-round magazine at 600 rounds a minute.

The shotgun was another great gangster weapon of the 1930's. It comes in various sizes: 12-gauge (bore in England) – barrel width .730 in; 16-gauge (.662 in); 20 gauge (.615 in) and 410 (.410 in). There are single-barrel one-shots, twin-barrel side-by-sides, twin "over-and-under" models; single-barrel "slide" repeaters and single-barrel semi-automatics.

Up to 20 yards the Chicago shotgun was sheer murder. On a 12-gauge the average load is one ounce of 6-shot size – about 400 separate balls. The "shot" spreads in a cone when the gun is fired. Illegally, gangsters used to cut about a foot off the barrel, which gave a greater spread of shot at close range; hence the term: "sawn-off shotgun".

The Smith and Wesson .38 revolver, standard issue for the British Army in World War II, is also a favourite hand-gun, particularly among police forces. It fires six shots and is, of course, a close-range weapon. (Remember the line of dialogue from *Dr. No*, when Bond deliberately lets his opponent expend six useless shots – then quite coldly shoots him with the remark: "That was a Smith and Wesson, doc – you've had your six.")

Webley also make a .38 six-shot revolver, with barrel lengths of three, four and five inches. The three-inch job, fitted with a smaller grip, is officially known as the "pocket model"; generally, this is the .38 "snub-nosed police special" used in movies.

Private eyes in films seem to equip themselves with the Browning 9 mm. Parabellum high-power automatic pistol, carrying a 13-shot magazine. The Luger automatic, another favourite, fires 7.65 mm ammunition, has an eight-shot magazine and is accurate up to 75 yards.

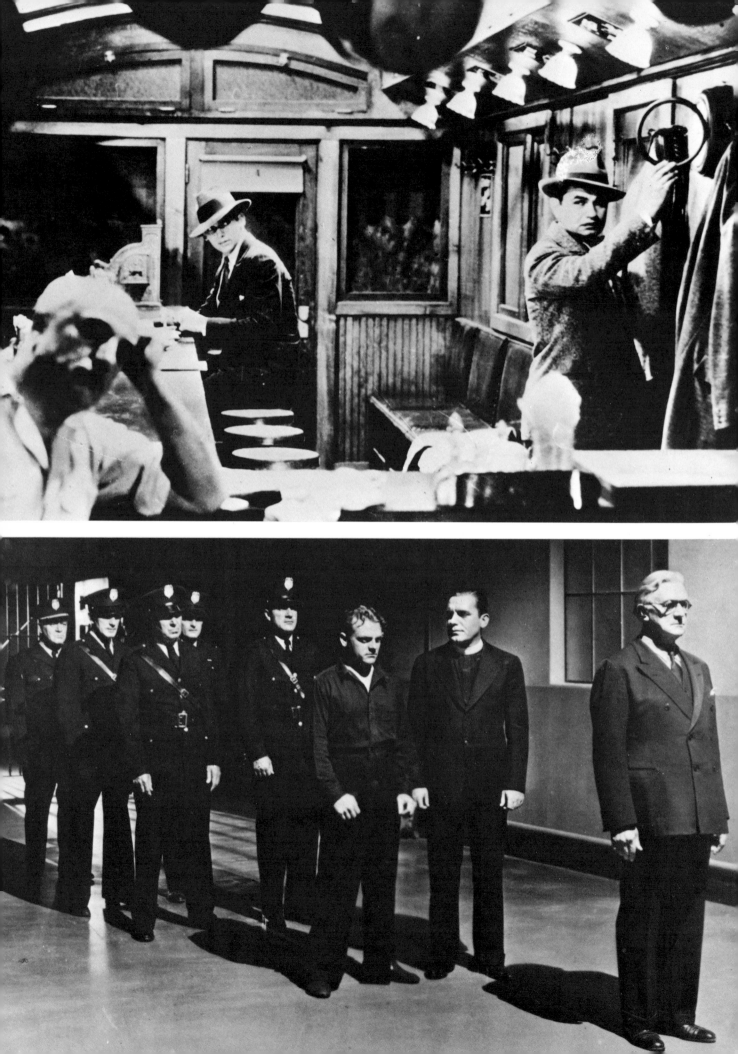

THE LITTLE CAESARS

WHO ARE the Little Caesars of the screen? Bogart, Robinson, Cagney, Ladd, Raft, Palance, Steiger, Duryea, Rooney, Bickford, Arnold, Marvin, Lancaster, Gable, Tracy . . . you could never come to the end of the list. Gangsters, hoodlums, mobsters, gunmen and tough guys all, and it's now more than 40 years since they went on the rampage.

Since 1931, when screen gangsterism first sold tickets at the box-office, the cry has been raised at regular intervals: "The gangster film is dead!" No matter how often this charge has been heard, the gangster movie has always managed to resurrect itself, Phoenix-like, from the ashes of its own violence.

By 1934, the gangster film had temporarily run its course. There were two reasons for this. One was that the public was tired of seeing films which were virtually remakes of *Little Caesar*. It has always been that way in the film industry. One company makes a hit with a particular type of story, and immediately everyone tries to jump on the bandwagon . . . until the springs break.

The other reason was that the earliest of these films of violence somehow managed to glorify the gangster, despite the fact that virtue was triumphant in the last reel. Protests rolled in from all over the U.S.A., the most important of all Hollywood's markets. The Hays Office, with its finger firmly on the pulse of public opinion, could sense that a boycott of gangster films – and not only that, a rejection of all film product from the offending studios – might occur throughout America.

The times, too, were changing. Prohibition was repealed at the end of 1933; bootlegging was finished as big business. Al Capone was on his way to jail for income-tax evasion. The real-life gangster was already turning to other methods of making a dishonest dollar.

But the screen gangster was by no means dead. By 1936, a different kind of mobster movie was on its way to success. Humphrey Bogart, lisping and snarling behind a three-day growth of beard,

played Duke Mantee in *The Petrified Forest* and scared audiences out of their tip-up seats.

There was, however, a difference. Duke Mantee was a killer on the run. He was not a big-shot businessman. The assumption put into the audience's mind was that this mobster was a bank robber, a hold-up artist, an escaped convict . . . but never a wealthy criminal controlling an empire of corruption from plush offices on the 18th floor.

It didn't last, of course. Warner Brothers, who had launched the cycle in the first place, were never a company to pass up a good thing. They saw how successful the Goldwyn film of *Dead End*, a long-running Broadway play, had been in 1937, and how the six Dead End Kids had scored a tremendous personal triumph in the picture. And they had a stable of contract artistes who were ready-made for the hoodlum business.

The result was *Angels With Dirty Faces* in 1938: Jimmy Cagney and Pat O'Brien, with the Dead End Kids, plus – for good measure – Humphrey Bogart, in a movie about how gangsters used to be. It was a fairly routine plot. Two young men of the 1920's, one of whom (O'Brien) becomes a priest, the other of whom (Cagney) goes in for bootlegging. Cagney and O'Brien set one another off perfectly, and the film had a twist which made everything all right with the censors.

Cagney, sentenced to the electric chair for murder, is defiant almost to the end. He's not going to break down and plead for mercy. To the Dead End Kids, he's still a hero . . . which gives Father O'Brien something of a problem. Even that final chat in the Death Cell appears to leave Cagney unrepentant. Then, as he is marched to the death house, a different Cagney emerges. He collapses, he becomes a screaming coward. He goes to electrocution in abject fear. The Dead End Kids see their hero destroyed, but the audience knows better. It's all an act; Cagney is doing his last good turn for Father O'Brien.

By 1939, Cagney was back with Bogart in *The*

ABOVE LEFT *Edward G. Robinson playing with time in the famous* Little Caesar *(First National 1931)*
BELOW LEFT *"Cagney, sentenced to the electric chair for murder, is defiant almost to the end" in* Angels with Dirty Faces *(WB 1938)*

TOP *In* Angels with Dirty Faces
*(WB 1938) Father Pat O'Brien tries
to reform some junior gangsters*
ABOVE *A gangster killing in* Murder
Incorporated *(Princess Prod. Corp./
20th Century-Fox 1960)*
RIGHT *The unmistakeable face of
Cagney in* The Roaring Twenties
(Warners 1939)
FAR RIGHT *George Segal (left) and
David Canary (right) in* The St.
Valentine's Day Massacre *(Los
Altos/20th Century-Fox 1967)*

Three scenes from the exciting Salzburg Connection *(Inigo Preminger 1972)*
which starred Barry Newman and Anna Karina

31

In Magnum Force *(Malpaso 1973) three cops* (above) *tried to enforce their own brand of law, but were thwarted by unorthodox lawman, Clint Eastwood* (below), *here seen with Felton Perry*
FAR RIGHT *Steve McQueen plays a tough character in* Getaway *(Astral/Foster-Brower for National General 1972)*

Roaring Twenties ... and guess who's producing it? Warner Brothers/First National, of course, from a story by Mark Hellinger. The director was Raoul Walsh, an odd choice for what turned out to be a first-rate action film, for Walsh was not normally a crime-film director. Gangsters could now be presented as history, and everyone knows just how violent history can be.

Because of World War II, mobsterism suffered a decline in favour of musicals and on-to-Tokyo epics. There was, however, one routine Bogart programme, called *All Through The Night* in which, as a racketeer, he comes up against Nazi spies and prefers patriotism to the profits of crime. It is memorable for one thing; the moment when Bogie threatens a nasty Nazi and Bogie's henchman – the derby-topped Ed Brophy, raps out: "You hoid what de man said. Why don't you do what de man says?"

Big-time crime returned in 1945, when Lawrence Tierney played Dillinger in the film of that name. It was followed by a number of gangster biographies like *Al Capone, The Scarface Mob, The Legs Diamond Story*, and others. During the 1950's a new wave of hoodlum pictures also filled the screens: *The Asphalt Jungle, The Big Heat, Rogue Cop, Party Girl, The Desperate Hours*, to name but five.

Again the times were changing, and with them came a totally new kind of mobster movie. It began with *Bonnie and Clyde* in 1967 – not a film about gangsters of the Capone pattern, but a story about two real people of the roaring '20's who carved a swathe of bank robberies and murders across the south-west of America. It showed a new kind of violence in which people could be hurt by guns; when Bonnie (Faye Dunaway) is shot to death in the last reel, it really looks as though heavy duty bullets are ripping into her.

Bonnie and Clyde, however, managed to convey the impression that these two youngsters enjoyed themselves robbing banks and stores. It also implied that it was very easy for them to fool the law – as certainly happened in real life. Though retribution caught up with them, audiences chuckled at their exploits (perhaps because the car chases were counterpointed by jolly, tinkling, barrelhouse piano music?) and wanted them to escape.

Since then, the screen has enlarged upon this violent mood. Censorship, too, has relaxed both in Britain and America. Today it is possible for the bad guys to dodge their just deserts – something which could never have happened even in the times of *Scarface* and *Public Enemy*. In *Getaway*, Steve

McQueen and Ali MacGraw rob banks and shoot people. Honest citizens are terrorized. No one could possibly say that either McQueen or Mac-Graw is a nice character, yet audience sympathy is awakened for them, and at the end they ride off happily to spend their ill-gotten gains. When Lee Marvin goes on the rampage in *Point Blank*, he is not a good guy searching out wrongdoers, but a bad guy revenging himself on guys who are worse than himself. Again, in *Prime Cut*, he is a hired gun in the present day who ruthlessly carves his way through Kansas. Both times, he gets away with it.

The Godfather must also fall into this new category of gangster films. Because much of it is presented as near-history, it gets away with an unprecedented amount of violence, and none of the Mafia characters in it ever gets arrested for murder. At the end, the new Godfather (Al Pacino) is a respectable husband and father, head of a big business allied to crime; the only punishment which may come to him is in his own mind ... and this does not seem likely to happen. The gangster movie has completed a circle and is once again portraying hoodlums as the central characters; this time, however, they don't have to take the rap to please the censor.

So let's look at some of the screen mobsters in close-up. Who are the Little Caesars and their descendants?

Who Played The Mobsters?

Al Capone was "The Big Fellow", so it's only right that he should have been portrayed on screen more times than any of his contemporaries. Here's a list of screen Capones or near-Capones:

Paul Muni	Scarface (1931)
Edward G. Robinson	Little Caesar
Wallace Beery	The Secret Six
Neville Brand	The Scarface Mob
Rod Steiger	Al Capone
Barry Sullivan	The Gangster
Jason Robards	The St. Valentine's Day Massacre

But there were other gangsters, gunmen and hoodlums of the era who have also won a share of screen fame.

"Little Hymie" Weiss, for instance. He took over control of the Dion O'Banion gang after O'Banion was rubbed out in his flower shop at 738 North State Street, Chicago. This was the famous handshake murder, in which O'Banion's gun-hand was gripped in a firm handshake by one man while two others pumped six shots into him.

James Cagney played a character based on Weiss in *Public Enemy*. In later years, Cagney also played the role of another famous gangster who became the manager of singer Ruth Etting, in a film called *Love Me or Leave Me*.

ABOVE *Paul Muni on the offensive in* Scarface *(UA 1932)*
RIGHT *Four faces of Capone. Neville Brand* (above right), *a pretty good Capone, makes with the dames in* The Scarface Mob *(Desilu 1959). Rod Steiger* (above far right) *played "Big Al", scar and all, in* Al Capone *(Burrows-Ackerman-Allied Artists 1958). The real Capone was never photographed from this side. Jason Robards* (right) *with another Capone portrayal in* The St. Valentine's Day Massacre *(Los Altos/20th Century-Fox 1967), and goodlooking Barry Sullivan* (far right) *as an unlikely Capone in* The Gangster *(King Bros. for Allied Artists 1947)*

ABOVE *Ray Danton as Jack "Legs" Diamond in* Portrait of A Mobster
(WB 1961)
ABOVE RIGHT *James Cagney played a character loosely based on Hymie Weiss
in* Public Enemy *(Warners 1931). This shot shows gangster high-life at its
highest, with Jean Harlow adding a "wicked woman" touch*
RIGHT *Doris Day and James Cagney in* Love Me or Leave Me *(MGM 1955)*

Ray Danton, of course, was Jack "Legs" Diamond in *Portrait of A Mobster,* and if the gangster-film revival of the 1950's had continued, he would undoubtedly have played many other famous mobsters of the period.

In the late Twenties and early Thirties, newspaper headlines were regularly devoted to the exploits of gangsters, gunmen and hoodlums of all types, from the big-business Capone figure to the hit-and-run bank robber. Of the latter, John Dillinger – Public Enemy Number One, he was once listed – has the strongest claim to fame.

Freed on parole in May, 1933 from the Michigan City prison after a nine-year sentence, he was 29 years old when he began to blaze a trail of robbery and violence across the Middle West of America. It lasted a mere 14 months, and in that time he was the cause, directly or indirectly, of 13 deaths; he also managed to steal well over a quarter of a million dollars . . . yet it was the fact that he went to see Clark Gable and William Powell in a gangster film, *Manhattan Melodrama,* which led to his death at the hands of U.S. Federal Agents outside the Biograph Theatre on Chicago's North Side on 22 July 1934.

A record like that made Dillinger a natural for films based on his career of crime. Promptly in 1935 came out two films: *Public Hero No. 1* and *False Faces.* In *False Faces* Bruce Cabot played the role of a bank robber on the run who undergoes plastic surgery in an attempt to disguise himself from the law; early in 1934, Dillinger had done the same, even to having his hands operated upon in order to destroy fingerprints.

Bogart had a shot at a character based on Dillinger when he played Roy Earl in Raoul Walsh's *High Sierra* in 1941. Ida Lupino was his hapless girl-friend. It was remade with Jack Palance, Shelley Winters and Lee Marvin in 1955.

Not until 1945, however, did a film biography of *Dillinger* appear, with Lawrence Tierney in the title role. Nine years later, Nick Adams became John Dillinger in a film called *Young Dillinger;* the famous ambush outside the Biograph Theatre was seen in *The FBI Story,* with James Stewart as one of the Federal agents taking part. Another Dillinger portrayal – by Leo Gordon – can be seen in *Baby Face Nelson,* for the infamous George Nelson was a member of the Dillinger gang in 1933.

Many other gangsters of those far-off days have turned up on screen. Among them was Roger Touhy, one of six brothers known around Chicago as "The Terrible Touhy's". They specialized in mail robbery and kidnapping, and they were

ABOVE *Dillinger, wearing a straw hat, walks into a Federal ambush in* The FBI Story *(Mervyn Le Roy/WB 1959). James Stewart is on the right*
LEFT *Leo Gordon played Dillinger in* Baby Face Nelson *(Fryman-Zimbalist 1957).*
In The Last Gangster *(20th Century-Fox 1945) Preston Foster played Roger Touhy (right). The other "Terrible Touhy's" (above right) were, from left to right, Victor McLaglen, Horace MacMahon, Harry Morgan, George E. Stone and Frank Jenks*

given film fame in *Roger Touhy, Gangster.*

Made in 1944 by Robert Florey, it was called *The Last Gangster* in Britain, and certainly it boasted an impressive cast: Preston Foster, Victor McLaglen, Harry Morgan, George E. Stone, Frank Jenks and Horace MacMahon, as well as Kent Taylor leading the G-Men.

A minor mobster who had a film biography made about him was Charles "Pretty Boy" Floyd, an Oklahoma hill-billy who became a hold-up man and was shot to death by Federal Agents before he was 28. The film, *Pretty Boy Floyd,* was made in

ABOVE *Jack Palance with Earl Holliman (left) and a young Lee Marvin (right) in* I Died A Thousand Times *(Warners 1955), a remake of* High Sierra

LEFT *In* Machine-Gun Kelly *(AIP 1958) Charles Bronson, no mean man with a gun or a dame, played one of the gangsters of the 1930's*

ABOVE RIGHT *The four-door sedan is usually seen as the gangster vehicle in movies. On the right is what looks like an Overland; the convertible on the left is a Ford V8, 1933 vintage. Mickey Rooney bites the dust and Carolyn Jones comforts, in* Baby Face Nelson *(Fryman-Zimbalist 1957)*

RIGHT A House is Not a Home *(Embassy 1964) was based on the life of Polly Adler, New York bordello-keeper de luxe in the 1930's*

FAR RIGHT *The end of the road for Dutch Schultz (Vic Morrow) and another gangster, in* Portrait of A Mobster *(WB 1961)*

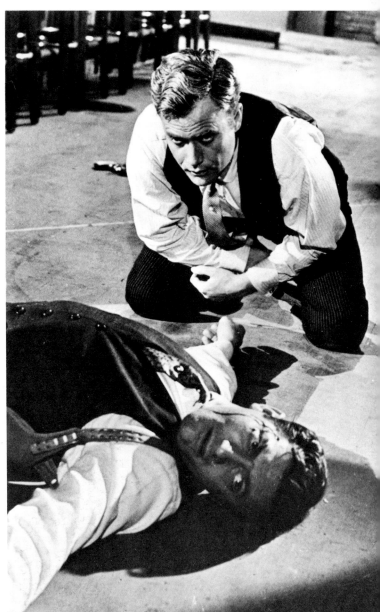

ABOVE *Contemporary newspaper report of the death of Bonnie Parker and Clyde Barrow*

1959 and featured John Ericson in the title role. Perhaps more attention was paid in the 1930's to "Pretty Boy" than he deserved; nevertheless, the *New York Times* took the trouble to print an obituary which commented: ". . . it was said that he was fearless and a good shot, an amazingly skilled automobile driver, a killer, and a man with a quaint pride in the fact that his robbery victims were generally rich." Perhaps, too, Charles Floyd sensed his own doom: in a badly-typed letter to a newspaper he wrote: "Thanks for the compliments and the pictures of me in your paper. I'll be gone when you get this. Jesse James was no punk himself. I'm not as bad as they say I am. They just wouldn't let me alone after I got out."

It would be churlish not to mention the exploits of Bonnie Parker and Clyde Barrow, as brought to the screen by Faye Dunaway and Warren Beatty. *Bonnie and Clyde*, however, was not the first film about this rather unpleasant young couple, whose real-life exploits were considerably more tawdry than they appeared in the film.

One earlier version was *Guns Don't Argue*, with Jean Harvey playing Bonnie. This was in 1955. Three years later came *The Bonnie Parker Story*, in which Dorothy Provine was Bonnie, backed up by Jack Hogan and Richard Bakalyan.

ABOVE *Jean Harvey played a gun-handling Bonnie Parker in* Guns Don't Argue *(AIP 1956)*
RIGHT *Two scenes from the magnificent* Bonnie and Clyde *(Tatra-Hiller 1967). Warren Beatty and Faye Dunaway in a shoot-out with the law* (above), *and the inevitable result of such a confrontation* (below)

A more colourful lady gangster – there's a paradox here somewhere; can a gangster also be a lady? – was Mrs Arizona Clark Barker, who certainly deserves the films which have been produced about her exploits. Born in 1880, she perished on 16 January 1935 in a four-hour gun battle with G-Men at Lake Weir, Florida. In her time she controlled a bank-robbing and kidnapping gang of at least 30 hoodlums; at various times her four sons were part of her organization.

Ma Barker's Killer Brood, with Lurene Tuttle playing Ma, was the first movie about the Barker gang. However, in 1970 Roger Corman followed the *Bonnie and Clyde* mood with *Bloody Mama*, in which Shelley Winters shot it out with the cops. Neither of the films clings strictly to the truth about the Barker gang; in *Bloody Mama*, for instance, the Barker sons last too long around the family table. In reality, Ma Barker had four sons: Herman was found dead in 1927, probably shot in a robbery; Arthur was sentenced to life imprisonment for murder in 1928; Lloyd got 25 years at Leavenworth about the same time for mail robbery. The last remaining Barker lad, Freddie – usually called "Doc" – was little known until the early 1930's when he joined his mum and an ex-farmhand called Alvin "Creepy" Karpis in the Barker gang crime wave.

Shelley Winters (below and far right) *knows all about killing in* Bloody Mama *(AIP 1969)*
BELOW RIGHT *End of the road for a playboy in* The Grissom Gang *(Assoc & Aldrich Co. Inc. 1971)*
Lurene Tuttle (below far right) *handles a mean tommy-gun in* Ma Barker's Killer Brood *(William J. Faris 1966)*

Echoes of Ma Barker and her killers can be seen in two films based on the James Hadley Chase thriller, *No Orchids For Miss Blandish*. The first was a British quickie which had more success than it deserved in 1946; Jack La Rue played Slim Grissom, Ma Grissom's sinister son, who kidnapped the heiress for ransom but preferred to keep her for more entertaining pursuits. The second "Orchids" movie was *The Grissom Gang*, produced and directed by Robert Aldrich in 1971.

One last famous gangster figure: "Dutch" Schultz, the New York beer baron to whose gang Johnny Torrio fled after deciding that Chicago was too hot for him. Poor old Dutch tends to get forgotten when talk of gangsters is bandied around, yet he was quite a character in his day. *Portrait Of A Mobster* (1961) was his screen biography, with Vic Morrow in the lead as Mr Dutch Schultz A. Flegenheimer. A year earlier, he had appeared in *The Rise And Fall Of Legs Diamond* with Ray Danton, who similarly did the honours as "Legs" in *Portrait Of A Mobster*. In 1964, Broderick Crawford appeared in *A House Is Not A Home*, a film based somewhat vaguely on the life of Polly Adler, who ran a notorious *bordello* in New York during the early 1930's. Though the Crawford character was not sharply identified as "Dutch" Schultz, it was generally thought to be him.

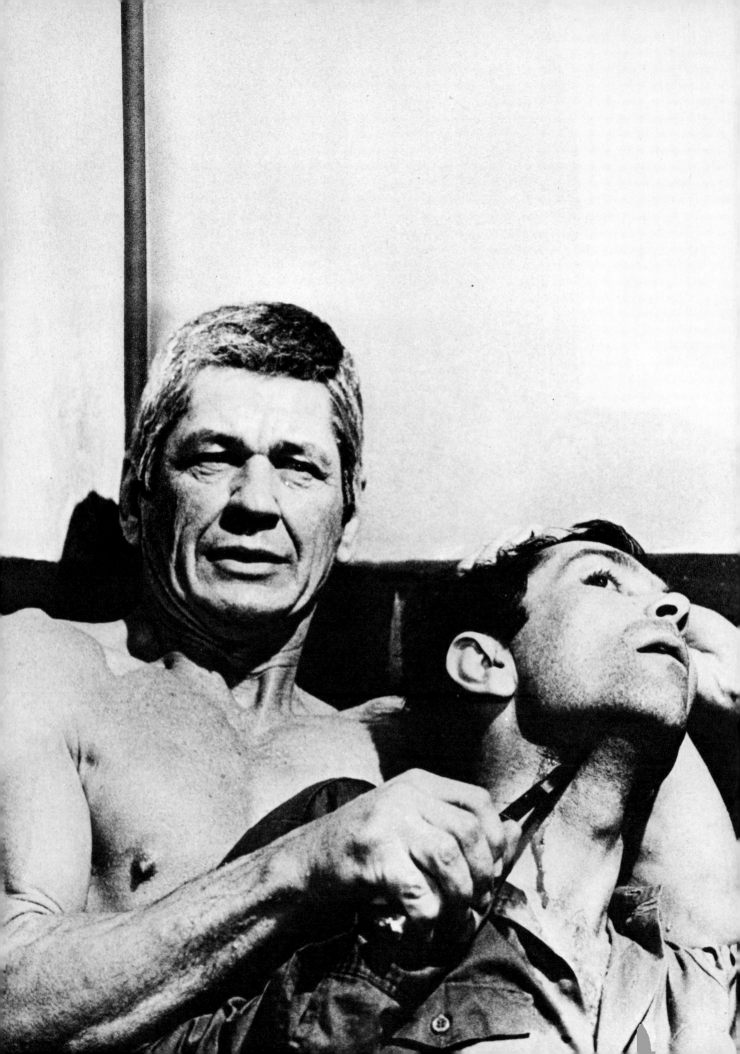

A GALLERY OF GANGSTERS

SOME OF the actors who have achieved fame . . . or should it be notoriety? . . . by playing hoodlums.

Richard Attenborough

Personally, I have never believed in Richard Attenborough as "Pinky" in *Brighton Rock* (1947). One is meant to believe that young Pinky – he appears to be about 18 in the film – is a cool, calculating killer with a sadistic streak and that the other members of his gang are completely terrified of him.

Somehow, it doesn't ring true. *Brighton Rock* is a film about the pre-war Brighton race gangs, who terrorized bookmakers into paying protection money for not having their stands broken up and their faces razor-slashed. A heavyweight book-maker would have just leaned on Pinky, so would the tearaways of his gang.

Still, it puts Attenborough into the gangster class. Later, he turned con-man – a very believable performance, this – in *Only When I Larf* (1968), and mass murderer in *10 Rillington Place* (1971). These days he is perhaps more highly regarded as a director than as a very good actor, particularly for *Oh! What A Lovely War* (1969) and *Young Winston* (1973).

LEFT *Charles Bronson is tough even when he's smiling. The guy on the other end of the point in* The Valachi Papers *(De Laurentiis 1972) isn't arguing*
ABOVE *Richard Attenborough in a scene from* Brighton Rock *(Assoc. Brit. Picture Corp. 1947)*

Warren Beatty

Clyde Barrow . . . that is the hoodlum with whom Warren Beatty's name will forever be associated. In his own production of *Bonnie and Clyde* he brought a depth to the part which makes it live on screen; that Clyde Barrow was unlikely to have such a well-rounded character in real life is unimportant. From now on, we have the Beatty-Barrow kind of folk hero in our mental projectors.

More recently, however, Warren Beatty became a slick bank-robber in *The Heist*. From the gigolo of *The Roman Spring Of Mrs Stone* to looting thousands from a bank vault . . . well, it's on the way up, isn't it?

In Bonnie and Clyde *(Tatra-Hiller 1967) and* The Heist *(Francovich 1971) Warren Beatty not only robs banks but also has a beautiful accomplice. In* Bonnie and Clyde (below) *it is Faye Dunaway and in* The Heist (right), *Goldie Hawn*

Jean-Paul Belmondo

France has produced many good screen tough guys – Delon (the French Alan Ladd, he's been called) and Gabin, the solid, heavyweight gangster are two who have become famous.

Belmondo is in a different category. He is tough, he fights hard, and he is a mixture of hero and villain. In *Le Doulos* (1963), for instance, he was an informer whom one never knew whether to believe. In a more recent film, *The Burglars,* he is certainly crooked, definitely a bit of a hoodlum . . . yet one cannot help liking him. There's a good deal of the Doug Fairbanks athlete-type in Belmondo, and this can be seen in *The Burglars.*

Jean-Paul Belmondo has a reputation for doing his own stunts, as indicated here (previous pages, above left *and* left) *in exciting scenes from* The Burglars *(Columbia Films/Video 1971)*
ABOVE *William Bendix (right) with Alan Ladd in* The Blue Dahlia *(Paramount 1946). Bendix played a character who didn't have all his marbles*

William Bendix

Bendix is the menace with the mostest. If there is a guy to be coshed or a hand to be stamped on, Bendix is your boy.

Probably he was at his most sinister in *The Big Steal* (1949), pursuing Robert Mitchum with almost Dostoievskian ferocity. There is something about that rugged jaw and brooding eyes which suggests the ultimate in menace. Yet, in *The Blue Dahlia* (1946) he was Alan Ladd's pal, the soldier home from the wars, the character who didn't have all his marbles. Maybe it is this combination of ruthlessness and innocence which makes him so frightening.

Charles Bronson plays a cold, dedicated "hit man" (above) *in* The Mechanic *(UA 1972) and an equally tough character* (below) *in* The Stone Killer *(De Laurentiis 1973)*

Humphrey Bogart

The Petrified Forest (1936) set Humphrey Bogart firmly on the upward path of crime. As Duke Mantee, the snarling convict on the run who holds up the wayside eaterie and puts the fear of the gun into Bette Davis and Leslie Howard, he created a character whom he was called upon to replay time and time again.

For several years he was the sneering, sadistic gangster, particularly in films like *The Roaring Twenties*. A more restrained performance was allowed him in *High Sierra*, where circumstances forced him – as a gangster out of jail – into falling back into the bad old ways.

Then came *The Maltese Falcon* (1941) and Bogie turned respectable ... well, almost ... as Sam Spade, the private eye created by Dashiel Hammett. In the world of gangsterdom, this was followed by his performance as Philip Marlowe in *The Big Sleep* (1946). Raymond Chandler afterwards said of him that he was the only actor who could be menacing without a gun.

Bogart made a great number of films but will be remembered for his fine performances in the above movies as well as in others such as *Key Largo* (1948) and *The Desperate Hours* (1955).

Charles Bronson

"Machine-Gun" Kelly was the role which gave him his first real opportunity to play a hoodlum; before that, despite having been born with the name of Buchinsky, he seemed fated to play Indians.

Made in 1958, the film *Machine-Gun Kelly* was produced and directed by Roger Corman for American International. It probably led to his part as one of the Western gunfighters in *The Magnificent Seven*, and from there to become one of the twelve convict-G.I.'s in *The Dirty Dozen*. He looks tough, yet manages to convey a sympathetic streak in the characters he portrays. In *The Mechanic*, for instance, he played the part of a cold, almost dedicated "hit man" who received his orders through the mail and killed only for cash; nevertheless, he was cultured, with a knowledge of music and art, and within his limits, behaved honourably.

"Machine-Gun" Kelly? He was a gunman from Oklahoma City whose main claim to notoriety came in 1933, through kidnapping a local oil tycoon for ransom. Caught by G-Men in Memphis, he was sentenced – with his wife, Kathryn – to life. An interesting touch, that. One somehow doesn't see Bronson dragging his wife around with him while he battles with the cops.

ABOVE *Humphrey Bogart epitomizes cinematic toughness. Here he is*
"persuading" Peter Lorre in The Maltese Falcon *(Warners 1941)*
BELOW *Bogie puts the fear of the gun into Leslie Howard and Bette Davis in*
The Petrified Forest *(Warners 1936)*

Neville Brand

It's a shame, but when you have a face like Neville Brand's, you seem doomed to play hoodlums and gangsters. And five will get you ten – as they're always saying in that kind of epic – that you wind up behind the eight-ball before the last reel.

Yet Brand – who has died on screen many times – cannot come to a violent end in the role which has given him a long run on television both in Britain and America: Al Capone in *The Untouchables*. He doesn't look a bit like Capone, but then, it's unlikely that Don Ameche ever looked like Edison or George Arliss like the first Rothschild.

In 1958, Brand was a really nasty nasty in *Cry Terror*, and got killed by Inger Stevens with a piece of broken glass. He was back to being Al Capone, however, in *Spin of a Coin* in 1961 when he played opposite Ray Danton. He went to prison in 1954 as the leader of the convicts in *Riot in Cell Block 11*, certainly one of his best performances. In 1962 he was again in prison, this time as a tough warder in *Birdman of Alcatraz*.

But he's really made for the hoodlum role. If anyone ever films the story of Tony Lombardo, Chicago Mafia boss in Capone's day, Neville Brand would be good casting.

Raymond Burr

Nowadays we think of Raymond Burr as nice old Chief Ironside in the television series about the San Francisco police. But Burr has had his wicked moments . . .

He is invariably a smooth, sinister heavy, rather like Laird Cregar, in whose footsteps he travelled before the days of Perry Mason. Observe his smiling menace in films like *Sleep, My Love* (1948) and *Walk A Crooked Mile* (1948). Watch him being crooked in *New Face In Hell* (in America: *P.J.*) (1968). Those big, melting eyes and that voice which sounds like strawberry shortcake . . . they can really scare you.

James Cagney

"Top of the world, ma!" That is a far better catch-line for Jimmy Cagney than "Yuh dirty rat . . .!" (complete with legs apart, hands-out stance), the line with which he seems forever to be associated.

Cagney is Warners and Warners are Cagney. From *Public Enemy* onwards, he *was* the rootin', tootin', quick-with-the-police-special gangster.

In *White Heat* (1949) he gave one of his best performances, typical of the Cagney character – the smart-talking, far-too-fast hoodlum on his way to the top as quick as he could make it . . . and in this case, it was the top of a gas storage tank, shot to death by police guns, and the tank going up in a blaze of flame while Cagney screams: "Top of the world, ma!"

PREVIOUS PAGES *Lee Marvin, a study in "hit man" professionalism in* Prime Cut *(Cinema Center Films 1972)*
LEFT *Raymond Burr doesn't look happy playing the heavy in this scene from* The Blue Gardenia *(Alex Gottlieb 1952)*
ABOVE *Get that pose! Note those hands! It's part of the Jimmy Cagney style, seen here with Bogie in* The Roaring Twenties *(Warners 1939)*

Lee J. Cobb

Controlled violence which is ready to burst into flame. That is the Lee J. Cobb gangster characterization and the one we have come to expect from this very fine actor.

Party Girl – it's an unlikely name for a violent movie, but it did nevertheless deal with racketeers. There's Cobb, flanked by John Ireland, pouring sulphuric acid on to a paper Christmas bell to let Robert Taylor know what it could do to heroine Cyd Charisse. In the same film he loses his temper and shoots holes in a portrait of Jean Harlow because he has learned she's just got married.

Cobb was also Johnny Friendly, the union boss-racketeer who came up against Brando in *On The Waterfront*.

It's rare to see Cobb actually being violent. Most times, he suggests the possibility of violence or that he will order an act of violence. His role is to sit behind the desk and make with the menace.

Richard Conte

Richard Conte's best performance – if I'm allowed a personal opinion – was in Lewis Milestone's *A Walk In The Sun* (1946). Not a gangster film, but the story of one platoon's attempt to capture a farmhouse-strongpoint in Italy during World War II. In this performance could be seen the background of a Brooklyn tough kid, dumped into the war, a kid who might have grown up to become part of the gangs.

That's what makes him such a good Italian-New York gangster (his father was an Italian barber). Films like *Cry Of The City* (1948), *The Blue Gardenia* (1963) and *Ocean's 11* (1960) gave him his chance at crookdom.

Yet he can be a sympathetic cop. With Frank Sinatra in *Tony Rome* (1967) and *Lady In Cement* (1968) he is the worn-down, overworked police detective. An actor from the city streets, that's Conte.

ABOVE *There is nothing very controlled about Lee J. Cobb's violence in this scene from* Party Girl *(Eurtepe 1958)*
RIGHT *Richard Conte (left) can put his arm on your shoulder and scare the pants off you, as this scene from* The Godfather *(Alfan 1971) illustrates only too well*

ABOVE *That famous scared look; Elisha Cook Jr. in* The Killing *(Harris-Kubrick 1956)*
BELOW *Ray Danton (centre) as George Raft in* Spin of a Coin – The George Raft Story *(Allied Artists 1961). Jayne Mansfield is on the left*
RIGHT *Broderick Crawford in* A House is Not a Home *(Embassy 1964)*

Elisha Cook Jr.

Poor Elisha Cook . . . he's always been fated to take the rap. A specialist in bell-hops, hotel desk-clerks and downtrodden underlings, Elisha Cook Jr. (what was Senior like, one wonders?) has carved a niche for himself in the underworld of film.

In *Baby Face Nelson* he got in the way of Mickey Rooney's tommy-gun when Rooney felt the need to demonstrate that this new bullet-proof vest was all it was said to be. *Hot Spot* gave him the role for which ever after he seemed permanently cast: the cringing, servile, ever-frightened clerk behind an hotel reception desk. In *The Maltese Falcon* he was the most inefficient gunman ever, letting Bogart take away two enormous Lugers and eventually being made the patsy for one of the many killings in that picture. He takes part in the racetrack robbery in *The Killing* and gets shot for his pains.

Only once does he seem to be getting away with it. Playing a Mafia leader in *Johnny Cool*, he survives to see Henry Silva delivered into the gangster stronghold.

Broderick Crawford

A little-known film called *Tight Shoes* has always made Brod Crawford one of my favourite gangsters. From a short story by Damon Runyon, it told of a gangster whose actions were mostly governed by a pair of overtight, over-fashionable shoes he had bought.

After that, I could never again believe in him as a tough hoodlum . . . though he tried. In *Born Yesterday* (1951), he was the semi-crooked scrap metal dealer who just "wasn't couth". He appeared in *The Mob* (1951) and *Scandal Sheet* (1952), and then in *New York Confidential* (1955), but it wasn't any good. Brod Crawford could be as beastly as he liked, but always I thought of him as a very human screen gangster.

Later, he became involved in a lengthy television series called *Highway Patrol*, in which he was on the side of the law as a police captain. From this he gave to the language the standard U.S. cop-radio code words for "I understand your transmission": "Ten-Four."

Ray Danton

It's time, one feels, for Ray Danton to make a Hollywood come-back. He was good, but very good, in *The Rise and Fall of Legs Diamond* – though this may have been because he looked as audiences imagined Jack "Legs" Diamond ought to have looked.

In *Spin of a Coin – The George Raft Story*, he was a reasonable Raft – if somewhat tall for the part – and managed the Guino Rinaldo role effectively in the *Scarface* film-within-a-film parts of the story.

Earlier than both these films, he played henchman to Mickey Rooney in *The Big Operator*, a smooth restrained performance in excellent counterpoint to Rooney's pint-sized toughness.

Jack "Legs" Diamond was a New York second-storey man – a cat burglar – who became a minor racketeer in the Dutch Schultz era. He has one interesting claim to fame: at his trial for murder, he was acquitted through what became famous as the "blonde alibi". His girl-friend swore that at the time of the killing he was spending the whole night with her. Nobody believed it, but the evidence stood up in court.

Burt Lancaster on the run in The Killers *(Universal Int. 1946)*

Burt Lancaster

Forget about Lancaster's long career in films since 1947; far too many of them have been Westerns, and they don't concern us.

Just one small role, in the first movie he made; the part of the victim in Mark Hellinger's first version of *The Killers*.

Since then he seems to have eschewed the world of crime, unless his convict days in *Bird Man of Alcatraz* can be counted. He was also on the verge of the rackets as the basilisk-like newspaper columnist in *Sweet Smell Of Success*, a film which did little business in Britain but which held all the nastiness of the Winchell days of column-writing.

Back to *The Killers*. Poor old Burt was rubbed

out for reasons that did not need to be specified in the film. It's a pity he had so short a life of crime; he would undoubtedly have made an excellent *Godfather figure*.

Ralph Meeker

If you like your roughnecks cast in the Mike Hammer mould (cast? No, they're hot-drop forged), then Ralph Meeker is the private eye for you. Some think of him as a hard-nosed version of Marlon Brando – Marlon's two-fisted younger brother, perhaps – and, in fact, he actually did follow Brando in the stage version of *A Streetcar Named Desire*.

But it is as Mike Hammer that he portrays all the unfeeling ruthlessness of the Mickey Spillane

Lee Marvin gets the twitch from Gloria Grahame in The Big Heat *(Columbia 1953)*

private eye. *Kiss Me Deadly* is the picture, made in 1955 by Robert Aldrich. If you haven't read any Mickey Spillane, the only way of describing this thriller writer is to say that he is descended from Dashiel Hammett with a touch of Harold Robbins and Hank Janson on the way.

Meeker can also be seen in *The St. Valentine's Day Massacre* and *The Detective*. More recently, he had a small part with Sean Connery in *The Anderson Tapes*.

Lee Marvin

Most gangster-movie fans remember that a girl got hot coffee thrown in her face in some film, but how many remember (a) the film (b) the girl and (c) the thrower? In that order: *The Big Heat*, Gloria

Grahame . . . and Lee Marvin.

Marvin is the ultimate in professional torpedoes. In the '50's in *Violent Saturday* he made a little name as the killer who kept using a nose spray while terrorizing Sylvia Sidney and a bank. When Don Siegel made the second version of Hemingway's *The Killers,* he was the cool, hard gunman who knew he was being paid to do the job and would definitely do it, come hell or high water.

His latest, *Prime Cut*, is a study in professionalism. Before that came *Point Blank*, in which again he was the unstoppable force. But watch him in *Prime Cut*. Notice the care with which he handles the tools of his trade, the carbine which takes to pieces and is lovingly kept in a neat executive-style case.

Edward G. Robinson

"Mother of God . . . is this the end of Rico?"

It's a great exit line, and Edward G. Robinson played it for everything in *Little Caesar*. He was the greatest screen gangster of them all, partly because he came to film fame with the first upsurge of mobster movies, but also because – playing against his true personality, which was mild and gentle – he portrayed viciousness and violence better than anyone else.

His list of gangster films is an impressive one. From *Little Caesar* on: *Outside The Law, Hatchet Man, Bullets or Ballots, A Slight Case of Murder, Larceny Inc., Brother Orchid, Key Largo, Robin and the Seven Hoods* . . . he really seemed part of the rackets. Someone once wrote that when Edward G. snarled, he formed his mouth into an oblong. Certainly, that cigar-chewing, sneering snarl became a trademark, along with a machine-gun delivery which was the joy of all stage impersonators.

Yet both the snarl and the highspeed way of talking were shown in only a few of his films – notably *Five Star Final*, in which he played a tabloid newspaper editor. Edward G. lasted so long in films that there must be many today who think of him only as the slow-moving, quiet spoken poker player in *The Cincinnatti Kid* and never as

Edward G. Robinson as a newspaper editor in Five Star Final *(First National 1931). His face may have been smooth in those days, but he was tougher then than in later films*

the mobster who used to rasp: "Okay – let him have it."

Mickey Rooney

If Andy Hardy seems an unlikely person to find in the hoodlum file, pause a moment and think again. Judge Hardy's little boy seems to have gone crooked around 1954, when he turned in a remarkable performance as a bent car mechanic in *Drive A Crooked Road*.

Cinematically speaking, he went from bad to worse in 1957 by becoming Baby Face Nelson in Don Siegel's film of that name. It's one of Siegel's earlier efforts, and in it can be seen a good deal of the pace and action which was to emerge most profitably in *Dirty Harry*. Rooney has all the cock-sure brashness of the Nelson character as legend leads us to suppose he might have been; in reality, Baby Face was a tough little hoodlum without the brains to get out of bank-robbing and into the more lucrative pursuit of bootlegging.

From *Baby Face Nelson*, Rooney went on to play a psychopathic convict in Howard Koch's 1959 remake of *The Last Mile*; Little Joe Braun in *The Big Operator*; and a crooked gambler role in *The Big Bankroll*. Recently he was with Michael Caine in *Pulp*, giving a beautifully overblown performance as a retired gangster.

As a gangster Mickey Rooney was destined never to win. But he parodied all the gangsters that had ever lived in his performance in Pulp *(Three M's/Klinger-Caine-Hodges 1972)*

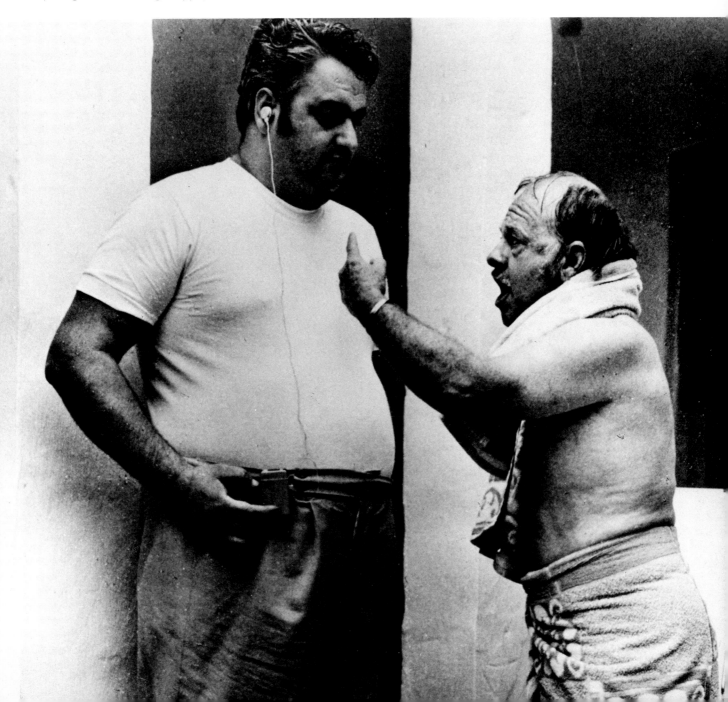

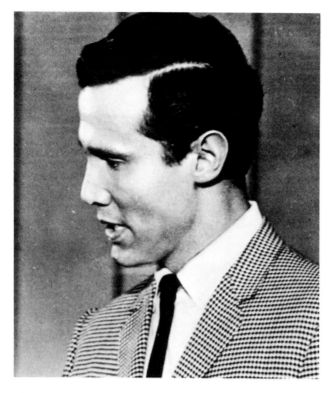

Henry Silva

Of Puerto Rican descent, Henry Silva merits inclusion in the list of Little Caesars for one film only: *Johnny Cool*. A William Asher film of 1963, it has been largely forgotten – yet it presaged the wave of violence which swept the screen in the late '60's and early '70's.

Johnny Cool is the story of a young Sicilian who is trained by his mentor (Eduardo Ciannelli) for one very special purpose; to go to New York and become a Mafia "hit-man". Once in the big city, he triggers off a one-man wave of violence in which his opponents – not enemies, because Silva is quite impersonal, as befits a hired killer – are despatched by gun, knife, rope and anything else that comes in handy. It's Bond-ism without the humour of Bond – and, inevitably, Silva is captured and condemned to a slow death in a Mafia basement.

The film ends abruptly at this point, and the impression is given that it was made as a TV pilot which could have become the beginning of a series on Johnny Cool. It was probably a bit too rough for its period, which may explain why Henry Silva now seems to concentrate on playing Mexicans and half-breed Indians on the Western range.

Richard Widmark

These days, a mature Richard Widmark can mostly be seen as a tough police detective in the *Madigan* television series, but there was a time, ah yes, there was a time. . . .

Back in 1947 he was a ruthless, psychopathic killer in *Kiss of Death*. Remember him in the train with Victor Mature, both of them on their way to the penitentiary? Remember that wild, maniacal giggle he broke into at the end of a sentence? If Widmark had stayed with this type of character, he might well have been good casting as Rico in a remake of *Little Caesar*.

Though he followed *Kiss of Death* immediately with the role of a sadistic (and crooked) night-club owner in *Roadhouse*, he reformed all too quickly and mended his ways with a succession of war epics and Westerns.

Madigan, however, brought him back into contact with the rackets, this time as a New York detective with somewhat unusual and extra-tough methods of crime prevention. Directed by Don Siegel in 1968, it's certainly a forerunner of *Dirty Harry;* it has also become one of the better American TV series.

ABOVE LEFT *Henry Silva in* Johnny Cool *(Chrislaw 1962)*
ABOVE RIGHT *Richard Widmark in* Kiss of Death *(20th Century-Fox 1947)*
RIGHT *John Wayne as a cop in* McQ *(Batjac/Levy-Gardner 1974)*

Two scenes from the very gripping The French Connection *(D'Antoni/
Schine-Moore 1971). Gene Hackman escapes death by inches* (above) *and
later catches up with his would-be assassin* (below)

In The Burglars *(Columbia Films/Video 1971) Omar Sharif* (above *and* below) *plays an Istanbul detective turned crooked and he is not averse to killing in cold blood to achieve his end – money*

GREAT COPS
AND
LONE WOLVES

THE DIVIDING line between tough cops and mad mobsters is often so slim it could be inscribed on the rim of a steel-jacketed .45 bullet. When Gene Hackman, as Popeye Doyle in *The French Connection*, is hot on the trail of that illegal load of heroin, he lets nothing and nobody get in his way. If one stands aside from the sheer excitement of the film and examines it dispassionately, it becomes apparent that here is ruthlessness which, under normal circumstances, would be regarded as the actions of a crazy man. Under the arches of the elevated railroad, the Doyle character drives a car like a character gone beserk; if the number of innocent bystanders sent flying and the total of wrecked cars were calculated, it might have been cheaper and more humane to let the villains – and the heroin – escape.

But . . . it's only movies. While the picture's running it is not necessary to wonder whether all this mayhem is morally right or wrong. Indeed, it would be a sorry day for the entire thriller industry, both written and screened, if ever we did!

This is a world of fantasy into which the audience is content to stray for an hour or two. There are the goodies and the baddies; the policeman may act like a baddie, but he's really on the side of the angels. It is a world of cops and robbers totally divorced from the local High Street, where we expect the occupants of the police patrol car to be amiable young men who stop for old ladies, collect stray dogs and take time off to give directions to Aunt Mabel's house in Rosemary Lane.

The really tough cop is a comparatively new type of cinematic character. When the gangster film was

LEFT *As Popeye Doyle in* The French Connection *(D'Antoni/Schine-Moore 1971) Gene Hackman lets nobody stand in his way*

OPPOSITE *The end of a great cop. George C. Scott, as a policeman who finds retirement lonely, goes out the quick way in* Precinct 45 *(Chartoff-Winkler 1972). In the United States this movie is entitled* The New Centurions

73

young, so were the policemen. That detective of the 1930's, Chester Morris – square-jawed and clipped of speech – might have knocked a hoodlum or two around in self-defence, but would never have been so careless as to shoot a fellow cop through being too quick on the trigger. Nat Pendleton and his boys might slam a quick right to the stomach of gunman Ed Brophy in *The Thin Man*, but it is necessary to look fast to spot it. The New York film cop of the 1930's would not have coldly broken a mobster's jaw, as Sterling Hayden did in *The Godfather*.

As screen toughness escalated with the gangsters, so it did with the police. Even the British policeman on screen today betrays touches of ruthlessness that would never have been allowed, in fact, not even considered, when the gangster film was younger. Sean Connery, in *The Offence*, is a detective-sergeant who has met too much cruelty in his career, and the horror of it eventually escapes from him when he beats up a suspect. That the man (Ian Bannen) is guilty has no bearing on the matter; at the time he is legally no more than a suspected person.

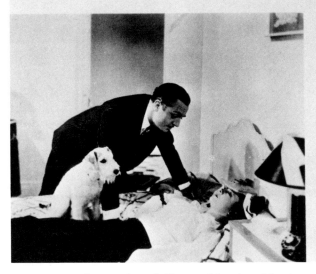

William Powell
Myrna Loy
in
"THE
THIN MAN"

A Censor Certificate.

ABOVE LEFT *Square-jawed Chester Morris, with tommy-gun, faces Lionel Barrymore across the table in* Public Hero No 1 *(MGM 1935)*
ABOVE The Thin Man *(MGM 1933) starring William Powell and Myrna Loy, marked the beginning of a new kind of private detective movie*
LEFT *The face of the cop. You'd never call this one "fuzz" . . . not if you wanted to stay in one piece; from* Precinct 45 *(Chartoff-Winkler 1972)*

ABOVE *Only half a baddie; Robert Taylor in* Rogue Cop *(MGM 1954)*
ABOVE RIGHT *Nigel Patrick was a cold-hearted spymaster in* Count Five and
Die *(Zonic for 20th Century-Fox 1957)*
RIGHT *In* Noose *(Edward Dryhurst for ABPC 1948) Nigel Patrick played
a Soho racketeer. The poodle, Nickey of Noose, retired to Cheshire after his
starring part*

Surprisingly, one of the best tough-cop performances in a British film came from Nigel Patrick in *The Informers*. An actor who has considerably more strength in this kind of role than all those witty, urbane characters in which he has found himself would seem to suggest, Patrick played a detective-sergeant with a genuine London accent – more Balham than fake Bow Bells – and showed a fierceness towards a gang of crooks which at the time (1963) was highly unusual in British pictures. It could be that the characterization was in a direct line from his Soho racketeer in *Noose* (1948), his cold-hearted spymaster in *Count Five and Die* (1957) and his police detective in *Sapphire* (1959). Somewhere inside Nigel Patrick, it seems, there is a Sterling Hayden trying to break out.

Town On Trial (1957) gave John Mills his opportunity to be a hard-nosed C.I.D. man, though not to the extent of knocking the opposition around for the sake of a confession. Matched against a murderer in one of the towns of Britain's

"stockbroker belt", he behaves towards suspects with the sharp brutality of a Chicago cop from the *Front Page* era. It is obvious that here is a Scotland Yard man who will let very little step in his way when he is after a criminal. He will bully and browbeat, but always within the law. The performance has all the elements in it of Barlow, from British television's Z-Cars series.

Movie cops can be tough, but they are rarely allowed to be crooked, and if they are, they meet their just deserts. Once upon a time, because the cop was also the hero, he was allowed to reform . . . usually through the love of a good woman. Of course, he would pay the penalty, but everybody knew it wouldn't be a long stretch, and she would be waiting when he got out. In *Rogue Cop* (1954) Robert Taylor was only half a baddie; he made mistakes, sure, but don't we all? That was the story attitude.

Compare this kind of story line with that of *Across 110th Street*, about a hi-jack of Mafia cash,

in which Anthony Quinn plays an ageing detective who has long ago sensed that all his efforts are not going to do more than lift the tiniest corner of the lid of crime. He does his job and he does it well according to his lights . . . but he is not above taking a bribe from a racketeer. His method of dealing with a reluctant witness is to slug him first and ask questions later. The strictly legal approach to police work, as exemplified by his opposite number, Yaphet Kotto – who also plays racketeer "Mr. Big" in *Live And Let Die* (1973) – is not for Quinn. This is his territory, his little kingdom, and he keeps the peace as best he knows.

Even Omar Sharif – an unlikely choice for a tough policeman, it might seem! – has recently played the part of an Istanbul detective turned crooked. In *The Burglars* (1972) he discovers a plot to carry out a big robbery and at once sees his chance to cut himself in for a slice of the cake. Whether he was "bent" before is never apparent, but from the moment he decides to blackmail the villains into parting with their loot, he becomes a one-man tornado. There is a scene where he orders his police escort to remain behind while he investigates a cellar alone. The crooks are there all right, but it is not his intention to capture them; he just means to force them to pay up. In cold blood, he shoots one of the gang to prove his point.

But police villainy must pay the price. At the end of *Across 110th Street* Quinn is shot by a sniper – one of the black racketeer's henchmen; Sharif perishes in a wheat-hopper as *The Burglars* finishes. Crime – as the old MGM series of shorts used to say – Does Not Pay!

One of the first – and also one of the best – films about the work of the ordinary policeman, uniformed and plain clothes, is *Detective Story* (1951), directed by William Wyler. Adapted from a Broadway play, it is in the *Grand Hotel* genre; it strips away the frontage of a New York police station and lets us see what happens to the occupants during the space of 24 hours. Kirk Douglas, riding high after his tremendous performance as a reporter in Billy Wilder's *Ace In The Hole* (1951), was one of the detectives, and his is a performance which is well worth watching.

Compared, however, with *Precinct 45* (1972), which likewise takes the work of a group of policemen and shows them in what purports to be their daily life, *Detective Story* is a restrained view of cops and robbers. *Precinct 45* is definitely George C. Scott's film; he is a cool, uniformed policeman who employs his own unique methods of dealing with petty crime – once again, it's the character who knows his beat and knows how to keep it under control.

Faced with the task of rounding up prostitutes in the local Red Light district, Scott is well aware that dragging them into court will result only in nominal fines and a great deal of wasted time. So he packs them into a patrol wagon and drives them around the streets for the rest of the night, thus losing them a night's earnings and at the same time keeping the streets reasonably tidy. He isn't in the least vindictive; he is merely keeping the peace in accordance with his own law. He even takes the trouble to stop the truck and buy them a bottle of whisky with which to while the night away.

ABOVE LEFT *Only one way to go . . . down. John Mills and Alec McCowen in* Town on Trial *(Marksman Films – Maxwell Setton 1956)*
In The Offence *(Tantallon 1972)*
Sean Connery (right) *played a detective who has seen too much cruelty. His equally tough superior was Trevor Howard* (left)

ABOVE *Joseph Wiseman, one of the best petty-crook players in film gangsterland, professes innocence in* Detective Story *(Paramount 1951), watched by William Bendix (left) and Kirk Douglas (foot on chair).*
In Precinct 45 *(Chartoff-Winkler 1972) the task is one of rounding up prostitutes in the local Red Light district (below); the star is George C. Scott (right)*

Yet this cop is a fast man with a gun. He is also the kind of policeman who is capable of administering a beating to the wrongdoer.

Tough policemen do not spend all their time slapping the villains around. Sometimes they are ruthless . . . and crooked, too . . . in more subtle ways.

Such a cop is the character in *Hot Spot* (1941) and its 1950 remake, *I Wake Up Screaming* – the American title of the original film. The story is that of a detective who conceives a hopeless passion for a waitress – hopeless because she, not even knowing he is a policeman, is terrified of him from the beginning. He murders her, then uses his police force influence to shift the blame on to the hero.

In *Hot Spot*, Laird Cregar played the detective – a magnificently sinister performance, though how

the New York police department allowed a detective as overweight as Cregar to remain on the strength, passes belief. In *Screaming,* the detective was more believable because he was played by Richard Boone, that gangling, fleshy-nosed heavy who did not become an actor until after leaving the U.S. Navy at the end of World War II, but who has developed into one of the best menaces in the business.

Among tough, crooked cops, certainly one of the best portrayals of all time is that of Orson Welles in *Touch of Evil.* The film was directed by Welles and, it must be admitted, horribly mutilated in the editing . . . though not by Welles. Playing against Charlton Heston as a Mexican detective, the Welles character – a bloated, dissipated, used-up police captain of a border town – will cheat, lie and murder in order to prevent the truth from emerging. It is

ABOVE *Three of the finest in* Detective Story *(Paramount 1951), from left to right, Chester Morris, Allen Jenkins and Mervyn Miller*
RIGHT *Laird Cregar, on the right, played a crooked detective in* Hot Spot *(20th Century-Fox 1941). Here he confronts Victor Mature*

one of the great *bravura* performances of all time, in a film which portrays a sensation of evil as no other crime movie has managed to do since. The gangsters – Akim Tamiroff and his screen family – are faintly ridiculous people who are yet terrifying because of the brooding menace they convey. Watch for Mercedes McCambridge in it . . . but look quickly, or it will be too late.

Of recent years there has been a tendency towards rough cops who are up against the system – whatever that is – yet who win through despite all odds. Richard Widmark is one of them. In *Madigan* he is a brittle, touchy New York detective who, like Quinn in *Across 110th Street,* knows the people on his patch and knows how to handle them.

Unlike the Quinn character, however, he is honest to the *nth* degree. He will kill, beat and cheat to destroy the big villains, yet retains a curious affection for the little crooks that cross his path. One feels that if Madigan took a bribe, it would be secretly witnessed and the evidence produced in court to the ruination of some baddie.

Frank Sinatra played almost a Madigan character in *The Detective*. He had problems in his home life, he had a girl friend who was not above letting him share her bed for the night, he was fighting against ineptness and venality in those around him . . . yet he managed to win through.

It sounds . . . well, yes, corny. It isn't. This is a classic formula for heroes, and it goes back to King Arthur and the Knights of the Round Table. Arthur was not wholly good. Sir Lancelot was not above a spot of adultery. Only Sir Galahad was entirely pure . . . and has there ever been a story about the Galahad character?

If, then, there is little screen value in purity, how does it happen that audiences are enthralled by the square-shooting policeman? What attracts them to *Madigan*? Why is Steve McQueen a likeable hero in *Bullitt*?

Part of the reason, it could be argued, is what might be described as "the 1970's face". One looks at Widmark and instinctively knows that this cop has *lived*. McQueen's rugged countenance is not that of the matinee idol; one accepts the fact that any character he plays is a man who's been through the mill.

As policemen, they don't have to demonstrate that they are above suspicion. Maybe their private lives aren't above reproach . . . but what does that have to do with their villain-catching abilities? Could þe there was something in the past which has led to their being rough and tough . . . but it doesn't alter the fact that they're dead honest about the job. In fact, the reason why Clint Eastwood behaves so ruthlessly in *Dirty Harry* is

carefully plotted at one point in the film: his wife was killed by a hit-and-run driver escaping from the scene of a crime, so he hates all baddies.

The strange thing is that many of these "straight" cops are capable of the most alarming acts in the execution of their duties. Take the car chase through San Francisco in *Bullitt*. No matter how essential it might be to catch the crooks in their car, it would be indefensible for any policeman to drive through city streets with such fury and so little regard for other traffic . . . and that brings us back to Gene Hackman's mad car chase in *The French Connection*.

The car-chase sequence in *Bullitt* is, of course, impossible – exciting though it may be. To film it, look-out men were posted at intersections so that the cars could career up and down the 'Frisco hills without killing off half the rest of the motoring population. For one set-up, the assistant director was compelled to lie down in the road in order to block traffic.

Since then, car chases in situations as close to

BELOW *Among tough, crooked cops, certainly one of the best portrayals of all time is that of Orson Welles in* Touch of Evil *(Universal Int. 1957) (U.S. title* Badge of Evil*). The Mexican gentleman is Charlton Heston*
RIGHT *Richard Widmark (centre) gets tough in* Madigan *(Universal 1968)*

real life as possible have become almost obligatory in the gangster picture. In *The Burglars*, Omar Sharif drives a Fiat in hot pursuit of Jean-Paul Belmondo through apparently busy city streets, up and down flights of steps, across pavements, anywhere and everywhere; it's great fun, but it holds up the plot for half a reel and has no real bearing on the story.

The latest in a long line of tough policemen is, of course, Clint Eastwood. After seven long years on the TV Western prairie, Eastwood first made his screen name in Spaghetti Westerns: *A Fistful Of Dollars – For A Few Dollars More – The Good, The Bad And The Ugly*. Then he moved into police films as the Western sheriff who comes to town in pursuit of his man in *Coogan's Bluff*, then on to the toughest copper of them all in *Dirty Harry*. As the billboards said: "You don't assign Harry to a case – you just turn him loose." The billboards were right.

Harry puts his faith in his Colt Magnum .44 and his ability to use it. When Harry points that hand-gun at you, either you give up or you're stone cold dead on the sidewalk. Don Siegel, who directed Eastwood in both *Coogan's Bluff* and *Dirty Harry*, has described policemen as "just ordinary people right in the middle of a very tough world and as insecure, faced with the contradictions of society, as the rest of us. The cop in my picture was a victim of violence in that he felt he had to deal with it with his hands tied behind his back. When he catches the killer using his own rules, he's in trouble."

Finally, the most unlikely tough cop of them all: Miss Raquel Welch. There she is in *Fuzz*, wielding a police special with as much aplomb as she might her eyebrow pencil. That the recoil would probably have put her flat on her back, doesn't matter; she is a dream of a tough cop. Like Madigan's purity, Cregar's weight and all those car-chases, it's just a question of how much the film can make one suspend disbelief. . . .

Lone Wolves

Mention the screen private eye, and someone is sure to bare his teeth and try making with the authentic Bogart snarl. Humphrey Bogart, the epitome of all the movie private detectives that have ever been.

Here's a little game to play when television palls. Ask half-a-dozen people how many times Bogie played Philip Marlowe, the private detective created by Raymond Chandler?

Next question: how many times has Marlowe appeared on screen and who has played him?

It's almost as good a game as asking who spoke the immortal line: "Play it again, Sam," in *Casablanca*. The answer is: No one. What Ingrid Bergman actually said was: "Play it, Sam."

For a bonus question, you can then ask your audience how the phrase "private eye" came into being. It's almost sure to stump most people.

Private detectives have been in pictures for a very long time. They were around in the early days of silent serials, when stars like Creighton Hale, Wallace Reid, Arnold Daly and Crane Wilbur were very gentlemanly private detectives indeed. They would certainly not have been referred to as shamuses, private eyes or gumshoes.

The Bogart kind of private eye developed on screen as a result of a revolution in detective fiction. He was born in the American pulp magazines of the 1920's and '30's, of which about the only one remembered today is *Black Mask*. Most of them were cheaply produced weekly or monthly publications, each containing half-a-dozen stories, sometimes with a serial running through several issues. Some of the writing was very bad indeed – about on the level of the worst kind of present-day comic strip. Raymond Chandler, truly the greatest of all writers of the hard-boiled detective thriller, once said that this was a kind of writing which "even at its most mannered and artificial made most of the fiction of the time taste like a cup of lukewarm consommé at a spinsterish tearoom."

Until then, fiction about police work was likely to follow the so-called "English" style, in which it was all right to be a private detective as long as you were a gentleman amateur. The hero could readily solve cases which baffled the bumbling flatfoots at Scotland Yard or the 53rd Precinct, but he was not expected to be professional about it and his only reward was probably in heaven. This was the school of "My dear chap, anyone can see that the butler did it, using a bullet made of ice fired through the keyhole from a single-shot ivory-handled pistol manufactured only by Dinwoodie and Wupple of St. James's." It was as artificial as a plastic lily at a wedding.

It was difficult for the silent film to be used as a medium for this "English" school of fiction, because so much of it depended upon a lengthy explanation in the last reel. Captions and titles were not suited to classic dénouement.

The coming of sound, however, gave some life ... though not much ... to the detective thriller on screen. Nevertheless, producers seemed strangely reluctant to draw on the deep well of stories which the pulp magazines had dug. Maybe they were still in a mental corset laced tightly by the restrictive influence of the "English" school – and it must be remembered that in the 1930's, deductive detective fiction was about the most popular form of escape literature throughout the civilized world. Maybe they thought the world market was not ready for the rough-and-tumble of American private eye stories on screen. They could have been right. Even up to the 1940's, it would have been difficult to find an English librarian who knew the name of Dashiel Hammett.

One of the earliest private-eye talkies was *The Canary Murder Case* (1929), featuring William Powell as an American detective called Philo Vance ... later described by Raymond Chandler as "probably the most asinine character in detective fiction."

This type of "classic" murder mystery, transposed to an American location, must have seemed a natural for early talkie producers: few sets, all interiors, a lot of talk and little of that difficult action stuff which meant the camera might have to move around. Like filming a stage play, in fact. Here was an opportunity to set up the static camera in its womb-like enclosed booth and let the actors get on with the job.

Most of these films turned out to be the dullest ever made. It wasn't the fault of Bill Powell, who played Philo Vance with wit and elegance. It was the fault of a basic misconception in making private-detective movies.

Powell played Vance four times. Others who followed him were: Paul Lukas, Edmund Lowe, Warren Williams, Grant Richards, James Stephenson and Alan Curtis.

Again, listen to Raymond Chandler: "When I first went to work in Hollywood a very intelligent producer told me that you couldn't make a successful motion picture from a mystery story, because the whole point was a disclosure that took a few seconds of screen time while the audience was reaching for its hat. He was wrong, but only because he

The Canary Murder Case *(Paramount 1929), featuring William Powell,*
is one of the earliest private-eye talkies

was thinking of the wrong kind of mystery."

That statement has sometimes been attributed to
W. S. Van Dyke, who directed *The Thin Man*, the
first private detective film to break through the
sound barrier. Conceived as an MGM quickie – it
was shot in 14 days – the film had the advantage of
being based on a successful book by Dashiel
Hammett, who had himself been a private eye. The
audience did not have to bother about who
murdered the butler with a sliver of ice in the
locked library: they were asked to be interested in
what was happening now, why it was happening
and sometimes how it was happening. They could
be just as concerned with the by-play between
detective Nick Charles and his wife Nora (William
Powell and Myrna Loy) as in wondering who did
the murders. For most of the film, in fact, the
audience is led to believe that Winant, the missing
inventor, is the murderer; only towards the end
does Nick show that Winant has been dead a long
time and someone else is doing the killing.

Another factor which made *The Thin Man*
notable was that Nick and Nora were – well, almost
– real people. Rich they might be: hard drinkers
they certainly were. They were a married couple in
the film, and they actually managed to appear to

enjoy it, making gentle fun of one another in every
scene they played.

Consider the first moment at which Nick and
Nora are seen in the movie. Dorothy Winant
(Maureen O'Sullivan) has seen Nick – who is
gently, but pleasantly drunk – in a bar. Worried
about the disappearance of her father, and re-
membering that Nick used to be a private detective
before he married Nora and her lumber mills, she
asks him to help. Enter Nora, with Asta, the wire-
haired terrier used to provide comedy relief. She
gets entangled in the dog's lead, is rescued by a
head waiter and led to Nick's table, where she
promptly orders five Martinis in order to catch up
with her husband's drinking. Then she asks who
the young girl is. Nick explains and comments:
"She's a nice young type."

"You got types?" asks Nora.

"Only you, darling," answers Nick. "Lanky
brunettes with wicked jaws."

The Thin Man pointed the way, with such success that five follow-ups were made, culminating in
Song Of The Thin Man in 1946. Yet even in this
forerunner of the hard-boiled private eye movie –
and Nick Charles, though suave, is a tough shamus
– the producers did not have the immediate courage

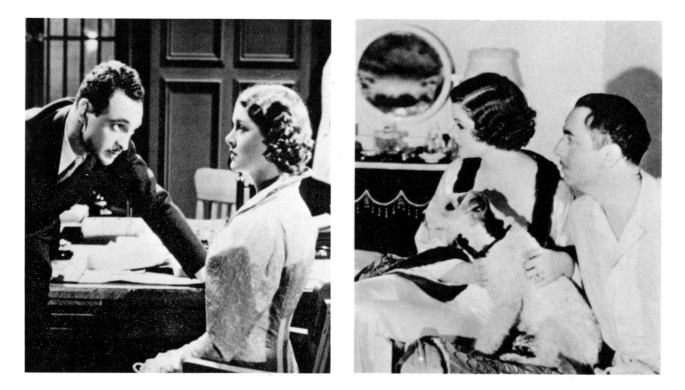

ABOVE (left and right) *One of the factors which distinguished* The Thin Man *(MGM 1933) was that Nick Carter and his wife Nora, played by William Powell and Myrna Loy, were "real" people. Five follow-ups to the film were made*

RIGHT *and* OVERLEAF *Frank Sinatra is a "jet setting" private eye in* Tony Rome *(Arcola/Millfield 1967), here seen with Jill St. John*

to avoid the classic dénouement scene – the one where the detective gathers all the suspects together and proceeds to unmask the murderer. In *The Thin Man,* Nick invites everyone to a dinner party and goes about the unmasking job as slickly as is possible; nevertheless, this final scene has something of the reach-for-your-hat about it. By then, however, the freshness of the rest of the picture had got most audiences so interested they were content to sit through a few minutes of who-did-what-and-with-what-and-to-whom.

MGM of those days, one feels, thought of *The Thin Man* as just a different kind of Philo Vance movie. Probably nobody in the studio had ever read any other Dashiel Hammett stories, let alone early Chandlers or copies of the old *Black Mask* magazine.

The Thin Man led Hollywood into producing other private detective films, few of which made much impact. Republic discovered Ellery Queen, the wealthy young amateur detective – he drove a Duesenberg, the most expensive (up to $25,000 in those days!) American car of the 1930's – whose father was Inspector Queen of the New York Police Department. In 1935, Republic filmed *The Spanish Cape Mystery,* with Donald Cook as Ellery; this was followed by *The Mandarin Mystery*

(Republic: 1936), in which Eddie Quillan – a most unlikely piece of casting – was Ellery. By 1940, Columbia had taken over the Ellery Queen series with *Ellery Queen, Master Detective,* and Ralph Bellamy – just right for the part – was in the lead. Later William Gargan, excellent at tough cops and hardboiled reporters, took over the role and was not really suited to it.

There were several films about Nero Wolfe, with Edward Arnold the first actor to play the part of the overweight New York detective who solved his cases without leaving his penthouse suite . . . a very odd way for a sleuth to behave! This was in *Meet Nero Wolfe* (Columbia); Walter Connolly took over the role in *League of Missing Men,* and in both films Lionel Stander – a gravel-voiced actor who now makes welcome appearances in European films and on television – was Wolfe's faithful assistant, Archie.

In the 1940's, Edward Arnold played a similar character in two MGM who-dun-its called *Eyes In The Night* and *The Hidden Eye* – a detective who deducted as much as possible from his armchair . . . because he was blind. The Swedish actor Warner Oland who had already made a name for himself by playing Chinese villains, abandoned

international skullduggery as Dr. Fu-Manchu and got into the private detective act with 16 programmes as Chinese detective Charlie Chan. The most memorable performance in these came from Keye Luke, an American-Chinese actor who was "Number One Son", though Benson Fong and Victor Sen Yung also appeared as Charlie's sons. After Oland's death in 1938, Sidney Toler took over as Charlie and made 11 Chan films; later an actor called Roland Winters became Chan for a further six.

There was even a series of Fox films about a Japanese detective called Mr. Moto, with Peter Lorre in the name part between 1937 and 1939. For obvious reasons connected with World War II, Mr. Moto faded from the screen after that. About the same time, Boris Karloff appeared in several pictures for Monogram, playing another Oriental detective, Mr. Wong.

Largely, however, these movies are forgotten. MGM tried to keep the private eye going in 1939 with *Nick Carter, Master Detective,* in which Walter Pidgeon played the detective about whom various stories had been written since the turn of the century.

Still to come, however, was Chandler's world of the man who is a private detective because that happens to be the way in which he makes his living, a world "in which gangsters can rule nations and almost rule cities . . . in which a screen star can be the finger man for a mob . . . where the mayor of your town may have condoned murder as an instrument of money-making, where no man can walk down a dark street in safety because law and order are things we talk about but refrain from practising . . ."

When John Huston made *The Maltese Falcon* in 1941, the detective film of the amateurish private eye, together with the film of pure deduction, became overnight as dead as silent movies.

Warners had made two previous attempts to film the story, in 1931 and 1936. The first of these, also called *The Maltese Falcon,* featured Ricardo Cortez as Sam Spade, with Bebe Daniels as Brigid and Dudley Digges as Gutman, the fat man. An interesting piece of casting in this version is that of an actor now seemingly forgotten: Dwight Frye, who had played Renfield, the fly-eating victim of the vampire, in the first *Dracula,* was Wilmer, the gunsel sidekick of Gutman.

In the 1936 version the plot was turned upside down. The jewelled falcon became a diamond-studded horn, and Gutman was turned into a fat lady, played by Alison Skipworth. Warren

LEFT *Jump for your life! An athletic Burt Reynolds in* Shamus *(Columbia/ Westman 1972)*

ABOVE *Ah . . . a clue! Walter Pidgeon, with a hacksaw, spots the vital link in* Nick Carter, Master Detective *(MGM 1939)*

William was Spade and Bette Davis played the Mary Astor role. Even the title went; the film became *Satan Met A Lady*. It could not be said to have added anything to the Hammett novel.

Viewed today, Huston's version of *The Maltese Falcon* seems strangely old-fashioned. The laconic, tough private eye; the bloated villain; the friendly cop and his brutal Number Two; the heroine who is certainly not as white as snow.

"Haven't we seen all this before?" is the question that immediately springs to mind. Of course we have, all too often on television . . . and quite recently at that. Everything in *The Maltese Falcon* has been copied again and again to the point of exhaustion; between them, John Huston and Dashiel Hammett fashioned a new kind of detective movie.

The plot of *The Maltese Falcon*, if it is necessary to bother with the plot – for this is a private eye film of incident and characterization – is: who killed Sam Spade's (Humphrey Bogart's) partner, Archer (Jerome Cowan).

That, however, is the least important item in the film. The action is concerned with why Sydney Greenstreet and his minions are searching for the black bird (the Maltese Falcon of the story); what part the no-better-than-she-should-be Mary Astor plays in the search; who is double-crossing who and why; and how the hell is Sam Spade going to get out of it all without losing his licence and going to jail?

This type of confused plotting, with loyalties apparently shifting back and forth throughout the film, is what makes *The Maltese Falcon* memorable. Sam Spade almost sums it up when he points out, at one point, that part of the reason he's in business is that he is perhaps not as crooked as a good many folk believe. Maybe he is crooked. He bamboozles the police; he is willing to toss Elisha Cook Jr. to the wolves – "We need a fall guy" – yet at the finish he will not agree to the simple solution to save Mary Astor, who originally killed his partner. Private eyes, he says, are in business to solve crimes, and if a man's partner is murdered, it's necessary that he should find out who did it . . . otherwise it would be bad for business.

The road was open, though it was travelled infrequently until 1945, when Edward Dmytryk cast Dick Powell in the first of the Chandler movies about private eye Philip Marlowe.

There was an earlier one, *The Falcon Takes Over*, (1942) in which the Philip Marlowe character was adapted to become part of the George Sanders' "Falcon" series, but it is best forgotten.

A song-and-dance man, that was how the movie-going public of the 1930's and '40's saw Dick Powell. From *42nd Street* in 1933 through the various *Gold Diggers* films, right up to the 1940's, Dick Powell was the crooner who took the girl in his arms and murmured things about love in June. In the late '40's he tried to break away from the image (and who can blame him?), but it was not until he became Marlowe in *Farewell, My Lovely* (in America, *Murder, My Sweet*) that he established himself as a dramatic actor. Marlowe took him out of the Busby Berkeley routines and made him a hardboiled hero, complete with snap-brim fedora, belted trenchcoat and beaten-up roadster.

Farewell, My Lovely is great to watch, but almost impossible to understand. Even if one has read the book, it is played so fast that one can barely understand what's really going on. Particularly if one has read the book, perhaps, since the film strays wildly from the Chandler story.

It does, however, have everything which we have grown accustomed to in stories by a host of imitators like Hank Jansen and Mickey Spillane. Powell looks as though he's working for twenty five dollars a day and expenses; he looks as though he'll never beat the system . . . though he will go on trying.

Farewell, My Lovely has the added advantages of Mike Mazurki, playing Moose Malloy, the numbskull giant looking for his girl. "He was a big man, but not more than six feet five inches tall and not wider than a beer truck," is how Chandler describes him. There was Claire Trevor, a fading beauty married to a complacent husband (Miles Malleson). There was Otto Kruger, composed, articulate, and gloriously evil as a fake psychiatrist.

And there was also Dmytryk's direction, in which he followed the writing more closely than any other director of a Chandler story since. When Chandler writes: "A pool of darkness opened at my feet and was far, far deeper than the blackest night" – because Marlowe has been coshed – the Dmytryk direction gives us the pool, spreading across the screen.

Powell, as Marlowe, was followed by Humphrey Bogart. In 1946, Howard Hawks directed *The Big Sleep*, starring Humphrey Bogart and Lauren Bacall. Undoubtedly there was good reason for playing them together in this film.

A year earlier, Bogie and Bacall had appeared in *To Have And Have Not*, another Hawks movie. Though it was supposed to be from the *novella* by Ernest Hemingway, about the only thing left from the Hemingway story was the title and the name of

ABOVE LEFT *That famous Marlowe office. Client Mike Mazurki hands over
the notes to Dick Powell in* Farewell My Lovely *(RKO Radio 1944)*
ABOVE RIGHT *Sam Spade (Humphrey Bogart), on the floor, Elisha Cook Jnr.,
Peter Lorre and Sydney Greenstreet looking on, in* The Maltese Falcon
(Warners 1941)
BELOW LEFT *George Montgomery, playing Marlowe, gets slugged in* The
High Window *(20th Century-Fox 1947)*
BELOW RIGHT *Robert Montgomery as Marlowe in* Lady in the Lake *(MGM
1946). The girl is Audrey Totter*

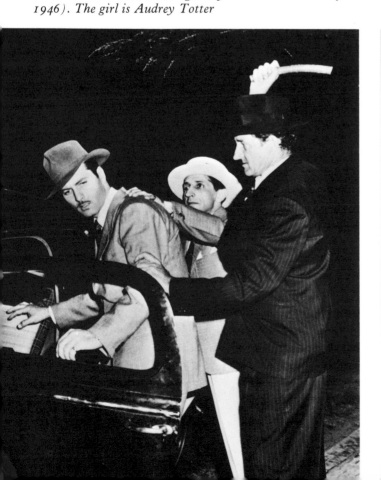

the Bogart character, Harry Morgan. Even then, Lauren Bacall relentlessly calls him "Steve" throughout the entire film.

In *To Have And Have Not*, the Bogart-Bacall team sparked off a kind of sophisticated male-female relationship which led to scores of copies in later years. Remember the scene in Bogart's hotel room, with Bacall poised in the doorway, about to leave and wanting Bogie to follow her. "All you have to do is whistle . . . you do know how to whistle, don't you, Steve?" It was the essence of the Bogart-Bacall relationship on screen, and the screenwriting team of Leigh Brackett, Jules Furthmann and William Faulkner refined it in *The Big Sleep*.

This was the film in which Bogart became Marlowe for all time. It was the only time he played Marlowe, but it stuck. (And that answers the question on page 86.)

Few of the actors who followed Bogart in playing the Marlowe character have succeeded as well as he. Chandler put it in a nutshell when he wrote: "Bogart can be tough without a gun."

George Montgomery tried in *The High Window* (in America, *The Brasher Doubloon*). It didn't quite make it; anyway, George Montgomery was too good-looking and did not have enough of the real Marlowe ruthlessness. Another Montgomery, Robert, made a brave effort in *Lady In The Lake*. He played Marlowe with the intention of making the movie a personalized "I" creation, as the books are, and was seen only once on screen, as a reflection in a mirror. In the 1960's, James Garner turned up in *Marlowe*, which was derived from *The Little Sister*. Most recent of all has been *The Long Goodbye* (1973), which has tried to transport Marlowe to the 1970's and – most Chandler aficionados claim – has failed.

The private eye on screen has joined the affluent society since the Marlowe days. Frank Sinatra, as *Tony Rome*, lives on a rather plush motor-cruiser moored off Miami, and manages to spend much of his free time deep-water fishing for marlin. *Lady In Cement* continued this saga of the rich, high life for private eyes; though Rome makes a pretence of needing the money, he never looks as though he would take a seedy divorce case, like Marlowe. In the opening to *Farewell, My Lovely*, Marlowe writes: "I had just come out of a three-chair barber shop where an agency thought a relief barber named Dimitrios Aleidis might be working." That would never be for Tony Rome.

ABOVE *James Garner among the dames as Chandler's detective in* Marlowe *(Katzba-Berne 1968)*
RIGHT *In* The Big Sleep *(WB 1946) Humphrey Bogart became Marlowe for all time*

Robert Bray (above *and* right) *as Mike Hammer, the "Spillane private eye whose sex life is so packed with incident it's a wonder he ever manages to call at the office". Scenes from* My Gun is Quick *(Victor Saville 1957)*

Another ingredient of the film plots which more recent private eye films have included is the element of: S-E-X. In *The Big Sleep*, the by-play of sexual feeling between Bogart and Bacall is suggested, never displayed. In *Lady In Cement*, it is implicit that sooner or later Tony Rome is going to get the girl into bed.

For this, the newer generation of hardboiled shamus writers must be credited . . . or blamed. Take your choice. Mickey Spillane is the man, and Spillane's private investigators not only move swiftly from fight to fight, they also barely have time to get out of a series of beds on the way. *I, The Jury* (1953) was the first film about Mike Hammer, the Spillane private eye whose sex life is so packed with incident it's a wonder he ever manages to call at the office. This was followed by *Kiss Me, Deadly,* in which Ralph Meeker played the Hammer role, and then *My Gun Is Quick* (1958), with Robert Bray as the over-sexed Mike.

Not one of them needs be remembered, except for the fact that in matters of bedding a succession of heroines, they set something of a pattern for future years. If one thinks about it, the James Bond series derives its sexual manipulations from Mike Hammer's lustiness; Matt Helm (Dean Martin), Harry Palmer (Michael Caine), Flint (James Coburn) and even Modesty Blaise (Monica Vitti), though closer to secret agents than private investigators, owe their screen sex lives to Mickey Spillane.

Nearer to the Bogart conception of the private eye is Lew Archer in the Ross Macdonald story, *The Moving Accident,* filmed as *Harper* in 1966 (in America, *The Moving Target*) with Paul Newman playing Archer, whose name was mysteriously changed to Harper for the film. How complicated do you have to get?

The Ross Macdonald stories seem to pick up where Chandler left off; they have something of the Chandler style, but without the brilliant, almost poetic imagery which Chandler could convey in two or three words. Harper/Archer is a Philip Marlowe type of private detective; he is human enough to suffer from indigestion, he has a wife from whom he is separated but whom he cannot forget, and he doesn't have much money.

Klute gives the private investigator yet another image, as played by Donald Sutherland. He appears to be so monosyllabic and so filled with sleep that one wonders how he ever manages to find his shoelaces, let alone a murderer. In truth, it is not really the detective's picture; the character on whom the audience focuses is that of the prostitute, played by Jane Fonda. This type of lack-lustre performance is again seen in *The Long Goodbye* with Elliott Gould playing Marlowe, and it has been one of the main criticisms of the picture.

But we can't have all our shamuses exactly alike. There's work for the tired gumshoes, as well as the hardboiled ones and the slick dicks.

A Spillane thriller which caused quite an impact, Kiss Me Deadly *(Parklane 1955) had Ralph Meeker* (left) *as Mike Hammer and Maxine Cooper* (above)

BELOW *Biff Elliott also played Mike Hammer in* I, The Jury *(Parklane 1953), the first movie about Spillane's private detective*

ABOVE *The computer-fashioned private eye of movies – Burt Reynolds in* Shamus *(Columbia/Robert M. Weitman 1972)*
RIGHT *Wham! Paul Newman delivers a telling blow in* Harper *(Gershwin/Kastner 1966)*

Albert Finney tried to prove this in a British parody of the private-eye movie called *Gumshoe*. It didn't work, for reasons which Raymond Chandler would be sure to have put his .38 police special on. The private eye doesn't happen in Britain; to be sure, there are private detectives, but those who try to emulate Philip Marlowe always seem to appear in court and receive a stern dressing-down from a bewigged judge. Probably the Marlowe character never has occurred in Los Angeles, either, but the genius of this kind of film is that it seems more likely that he does. Nor can the private-eye movie be parodied; perhaps because it already is a parody. We're back to that old thing: suspension of disbelief.

Latest in the long series of hardboiled private detectives is Burt Reynolds in *Shamus* (1972). As McGurk, a New York private eye who's afraid of big dogs and keeps a beautiful ginger cat, who lives in a single room and sleeps on a pool table, and who is quite capable of pushing a heroin addict's face into the garbage, he is certainly the 1970's version – almost in comic-strip – of the private investigator. He lives cheaply, yet is hired to pursue a theft of diamonds; he is big and sexy, and the gorgeous Dyan Cannon is only too happy to dally with him at the drop of a clue; and he is apparently so tough that he can take all manner of beatings and emerge unscathed. It is doubtful if he is the sort of man one would want to introduce to one's maiden aunt (the one with all the money), but he is certainly a character to fulfil all the audience's fantasies of violence, sex and thrills.

It is interesting to note that the highly artificial character of McGurk does not stem from a novel, but from an original screenplay. He's ready-made, packaged, computer-derived to fill a cinema need. He never ceases to thrill, but he is believable only

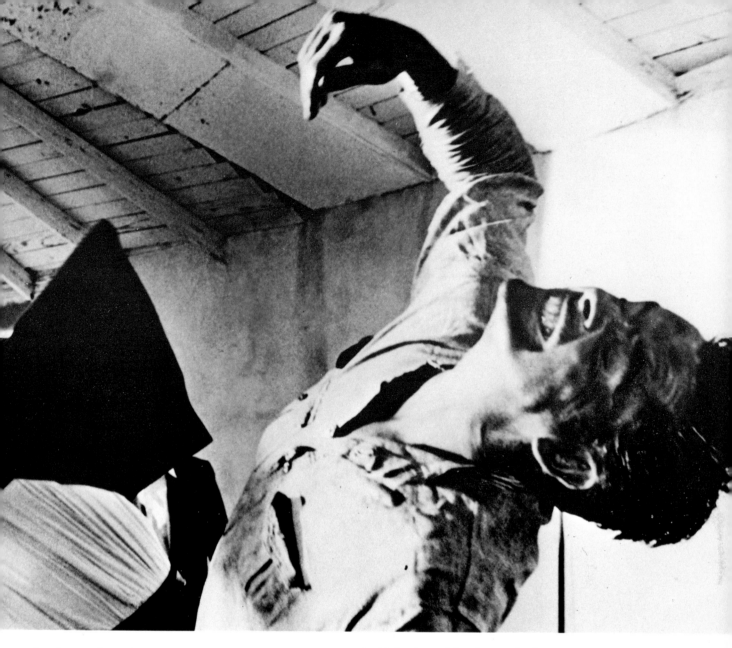

in cinematic terms.

Finally . . . black is beautiful, and with Richard Rountree playing *Shaft* (1972), it really is. Shaft is a negro private eye in the sleazy, downtown part of Brooklyn, and of all the new gumshoes trying to fill the Marlowe shoes, he probably comes nearest to the type of character devised by Dashiel Hammett in *The Maltese Falcon* and sharpened by Raymond Chandler in *The Big Sleep*. He is the kind of man of whom Chandler wrote: "But down these mean streets a man must go who is not himself mean, who is neither tarnished nor afraid."

If Shaft is ever afraid, he does not show it. He moves through city streets on foot with the lithe grace of a panther. He can hold his own with black man or white.

To the white police detective who looks sardonically at him and comments: "You're not so black," Shaft is quick to pick up a white coffee-cup, hold it alongside the cop's face, and reply: "You ain't so white, baby."

The mood of the film is set in the beginning when Shaft, striding along the pavements, is asked where he is going. "Goin' to get laid, man," he says without pausing. At the end, almost the same situation recurs. He is asked: "Where've you been, man?" and he says: "I've been to get laid."

The real point about *Shaft*, however, is that though the character does happen to be a black man, he could just as easily be white, red or yellow. Yes, some of the dialogue would have to be altered if he were turned into a Charlie Chan, but that is not at issue. There is a good deal of the Bogart characterization in Richard Rountree's portrayal, blended with a touch of the Paul Newmans. There is certainly no difficulty in believing in this kind of shamus.

ABOVE *A shot from* Klute *(Pakula/Warners 1971) that did not appear in the final picture. Jane Fonda is on the left*
BELOW *Sterling Hayden, Nina and Elliott Gould in* The Long Goodbye *(Lion's Gate Films 1973)*
Ron O'Neal and Sheila Frazier (above right) are the leads in Superfly *(WB 1972). Ron O'Neal is here seen (right) defending himself with a garbage can lid during a fight scene*

GOING FOR A RIDE

GANGSTER FILMS gave a phrase to the language: "Get in, bud. You're going for a ride."

Somehow, it has been accepted that this was the favourite method of rubbing out the opposition. It wasn't. Top mobsters were much too careful to be picked up in the street and herded into a waiting car; that sort of death was reserved for the individual who could not afford to be always surrounded by half a dozen henchmen.

But gangsters, and the movies about them, made audiences aware of the automobile as a sort of city streets combat vehicle.

And we must get the phraseology right from the start. In the world of gangland, the motor-car is an automobile. The black and white streets of movieland Chicago were strewn with autos, not cars. Brakes squealed on Chevvies and tyres screamed on Chryslers as those kings of the underworld fought out their wars at Milton and Oak Streets or along Clyde Avenue.

The car – sorry, the auto – and the gangster go together like Metro, Goldwyn and Mayer. They are as much a part of gangland as the tommy-gun and bootleg whisky. So it is only natural that the automobile should have played a leading role in most gangster movies.

LEFT *Gangster movies made the "auto" into a kind of combat vehicle for city streets. Still from* Dirty Harry *(WB/Malpaso 1971)*
ABOVE Ma Barker's Killer Brood *(William J. Faris 1966) . . . and this is the* Packard *to prove it*

From the beginning, with *Little Caesar* and *Public Enemy,* autos were used in action sequences. It was a reasonably simple task to post-synch the roar of auto engines and the shriek of tyres along with the chatter of the Chicago typewriter. Scenes inside the auto were more difficult and the tendency was to fabricate a studio mock-up in which the actors could be shot in close-up, cutting away to long shots of speeding vehicles, then back to the close-up interiors. Later, as back-projection processes improved, the camera was able to pull back a trifle and let the audience see what were apparently real streets outside the auto; the easiest method of doing this was to have the back-projection loop running through the rear window – often with the result that on a lengthy drive through a city, sharp-eyed filmgoers could spot the same point being passed again and again.

Also, because it was easier to confine the back-projection device to one window, movie gangsters tended to ride in sedans rather than tourers. The genuine gangster was more likely to employ an open tourer with soft-top raised and mica side-screens in place. This was to give protection to the occupants – you couldn't easily identify somebody behind those yellowing sidescreens – and also because the open car offered a wider arc of fire. It was a simple matter to smash through the mica and rake your enemy's auto from a tourer.

Al Capone eventually bought a specially-built Cadillac which cost him $30,000. It weighed seven tons, had a steel armour-plated body, a steel-clad gas tank, bullet-proof windows half-an-inch thick, a gun position behind the rear seat and a wind-down rear window for shooting at pursuers. And he normally travelled with one auto ahead and another full of gunmen behind. As a matter of interest, the Capone car is now owned by Salvador Dali.

But back to movies: in the silent days, before the restrictions of sound, the business of how to film with autos was not any great problem. The Keystone Cops, who invented the great auto chase sequence, were often filmed from camera platforms mounted on moving vehicles. Nor did the Keystone Cops suffer from traffic restrictions; they either shot without bothering about the small numbers of autos which then existed, or – if something really spectacular was required – they enlisted the aid of the real cops and had a few streets closed off. Life was simpler then.

Auto chases in the majority of gangster movies

up until the 1960's, though connected with the plot, were rarely a development of the plot. An exception is certainly Richard Quine's *Drive A Crooked Road* (1954) in which Mickey Rooney, as an expert tuner and driver who desperately needs the money, agrees to drive a getaway automobile for a group of hoodlums. The chase sequences are not all that good, largely because there is too much under-cranking, but the film has the merits of making the auto chase an integral part of the plot.

Not long after this came another auto sequence – not truly a chase because only one car was involved, but a fast drive along a cliff road on the Costa Brava. The film was *Chase A Crooked Shadow* (1957) and the car-driver was Richard Todd, playing a police detective who needed to put the fear of death into the hard heart of a murderess, none other than beautiful Anne Baxter. Again, most of the chase was in back-projection, but it did show that automobiles could be used as cinematic devices to further the plot.

Previously, Alfred Hitchcock did something similar in *Notorious,* when Cary Grant takes Ingrid Bergman for a hair-raising drive along the cliffs of Cornwall . . . though if it is possible to find such a road in Cornwall, the fact has never been revealed to the organizers of motor rallies. In this case, however, the Hitchcock intention was to introduce a scare-raising sequence which makes Ingrid Bergman – and the audience – suspicious of Mr Grant's intentions. Does he intend to murder her or doesn't he?

The true auto chase sequence as part of the plot came in *Robbery* (1967), in which director Peter Yates built a wild sequence with the criminals leaping, one by one, from a fast-moving Jaguar while being chased by British police drivers in the inevitable gong-clanging Wolseley.

Robbery is important, not only because it had one of the best auto sequences ever seen in a British film, but also because it led Yates to the direction of *Bullitt* (1968).

Bullitt first brought the auto-chase sequence to the attention of critical audiences and made them look back at Peter Yates' earlier film. This was a carefully-planned dash through the streets of San Francisco, with Steve McQueen as Detective Bullitt in a Mustang, chasing the baddies in their sedan.

For the first time, a minimum of under-cranking was employed, so that the automobiles had to be driven at full chat – as the race enthusiasts put it – in

A car has all sort of uses; scene from Precinct 45 *(U.S. title* The New Centurions*) (Chartoff-Winkler 1972)*

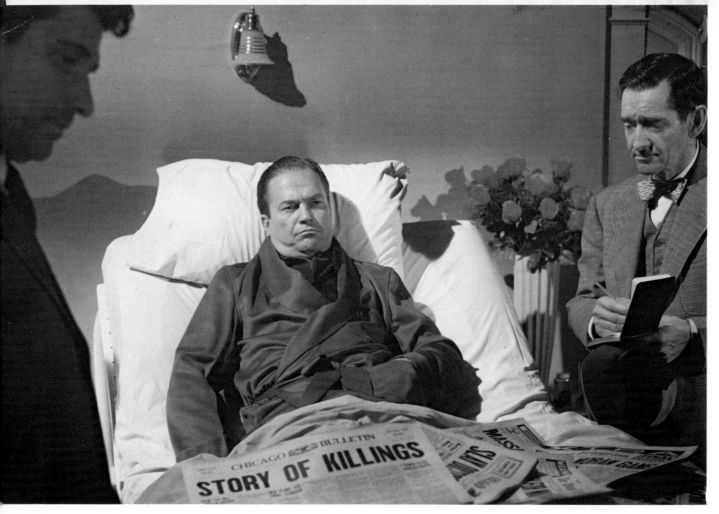

Three scenes from The St. Valentine's Day Massacre *(Los Altos/20th Century-Fox 1967) in which Jason Robards* (right) *played Al Capone and Ralph Meeker* (above) *played "Bugs" Moran, here seen in bed.*
BELOW *The gang plans its strategy on a craps table*

LEFT *One of the bent cops comes to a sticky end in* Magnum Force *(Malpaso 1973)*
ABOVE *The modern gangster has his autos customized; a scene from* The
French Connection *(D'Antoni/Schine-Moore 1971)*
BELOW *To get some of the low-level shots of front wheels twisting the camera
often has to be mounted in strange places. This is how it was done in* The
Burglars *(Columbia Films/Video 1971)*

*Thrilling auto-chases are almost a
prerequisite of modern gangster movies
as in these scenes* (above *and* below)
from The Burglars *(Columbia
Films/Video 1971) and* Penny Gold
(Fanfare Films 1973)
ABOVE RIGHT *The famous chase in*
Bullitt *(Solar 1968). Getting all four
wheels off the ground is called
"yumping"*
BELOW RIGHT *A scene from* Robbery
*(Oakhurst 1967) in which a "bobby"
tries to stop a getaway Jaguar single-
handed*

order to show on screen that they really were going
fast. Not only that, but in Steve McQueen the
director had a star with the ability to drive powerful cars very quickly indeed, and a good deal of
racing circuit experience to back him up. Therefore
Yates was able to use McQueen in many scenes
in which he would otherwise have been forced to
employ a double.

After *Bullitt*, it became almost mandatory for an
auto-chase sequence to be included in a cops-and-
robbers movie ... though not always with the
same degree of success.

The Burglars, for instance, has Omar Sharif
chasing Jean-Paul Belmondo through the streets
of Athens in what is quite a lengthy sequence. But in
the English-language version, at any rate, it
appears to have been included solely for the purpose of introducing an auto-chase; when Sharif
finally catches up with Belmondo's battered Fiat,
the pair exchange a few words and drive away.
Apart from this failure to further the plot, the chase
is very well done indeed, and at times the wildly
spinning cars almost seem to be part of an
automobile ballet.

The Italian Job, a British-made film shot in
Italy, is notable for the use of Minis as the getaway
cars and also for the introduction of a good deal of
humour into the chase. The Minis, driven by a
crack team of racing stunt drivers, leap rooftops,
drive across a weir and eventually garage themselves in huge pantechnicons while both vehicles
are on the move.

The weir scene is particularly good because it
shows that automobiles can be funny as well as
exciting. Hotly pursued by the police Alfas the
Minis race through the shallow waters of the weir
steps. As they dash away, one of the police cars
turns into deeper water and slowly – with appropri-
ate gurgles on the sound track – sinks into the river.
Macabre, perhaps, but it always raises a laugh.

As auto-chases grow more frequent, some actors
seem to become associated with them. Barry
Newman, one of the newer tough-guy heroes, has
had three in a row. The first was *Vanishing Point*,
in which he played the part of an auto-delivery
driver who decided to have one final, deliriously-
fast drive across the United States. There seems no
reason for it, except the sheer excitement of driving
flat out without regard for anyone else on the road.
Newman wrecks other cars as offhandedly as he
might throw away a cigarette, then drives his
machine into an almighty explosion. End of film.

He followed this in *Fear Is The Key* with a very
well-handled auto-chase through the Mississippi

swamp roads. Having kidnapped Suzy Kendall in a court-room, Newman is chased by the law; he not only has to keep Miss Kendall quiet . . . though at the speed of this ride it's doubtful if she would be able to do more than gasp . . . but elude his pursuers as well.

Finally, in *The Salzburg Connection*, Barry Newman is involved in another auto-chase, but this time with a distinct difference. The baddies, not strictly gangsters but hoodlums with Nazi connections, have kidnapped Anna Karina for some foul purpose and are driving away with her through busy city streets. Newman chases the kidnap-car by continually managing to get in front of it (the highspeed scenes), then slowing down to cause a traffic jam and attract the attention of the police.

Of all the auto-chase sequences used to further the plot, one of the most exciting – and certainly, one of the most beautifully-photographed – occurs in *The Last Run*. The story is simple: George C. Scott, as a retired Chicago gangster whose speciality in the old days was as a wheelman, lives in Spain. For various reasons, he agrees to drive a young hoodlum (Tony Musante) and a girl (Trish Van Devere) across the country in a getaway drive from the Guardia Civil and rival gangsters.

The twist is that the Scott gangster genuinely loves automobiles. In his garage he has a super-charged 1957 BMW 503, one of the prettiest sporting *equipes* ever built, and Scott cares for this machinery almost with the love he would give a woman. Forced to drive it too far and too fast with the "blower" cut in, he complains that it will wreck the motor . . . a thought about the internal-combustion engine which movie drivers never seem to have. When, at the end of the film, he crashes the

ABOVE *Auto-chase with a difference. Barry Newman uses his car to slow down the opposition in* The Salzburg Connection *(Inigo Preminger 1972)*
RIGHT *How to misuse a Mini . . . up and down the stairs in* The Italian Job *(Paramount/Oakhurst 1969)*

car, it is obvious that he will then sacrifice his life for the hoodlum and the girl, because there is nothing left for him.

Last word on chases: in *Puppet On A Chain*, based on the Alastair Maclean thriller, the Swedish actor Sven-Bertil Taube plays a U.S. narcotics agent investigating a gang of heroin smugglers in Amsterdam. Comes the inevitable chase sequence . . . only this time it takes place with speedboats through the maze of the Amsterdam canals.

Because speed on the canals is normally limited, special permission for the chase had to be obtained from the Amsterdam police. A full month of shooting was required for the sequence, in which two boats race along the canals, make unbelievably sharp turns and even jump out of the water.

The word is *unbelievably* . . . though that old suspension of disbelief is so well established that few audiences could have realized that seven boats and twelve motors were actually used up by sinking, smashing or general wear and tear. For boating enthusiasts: the yellow boat driven by Taube was a Shakespeare Sportsman ski boat, thirteen and a half feet long, built in fibreglass and driven by a fifty horsepower Mercury motor; the blue boat handled by villain Vladek Sheybal was a Eurocraft, also with Mercury engine.

George C. Scott at the wheel (above *and* below) *in* The Last Run *(MGM 1971)*
ABOVE RIGHT *A chase with a difference, in speedboats through the maze of Amsterdam canals in* Puppet on a Chain *(Big City 1970)*
BELOW RIGHT *The end of the road for this car in* McQ *(Batjac/Levy-Gardner 1974), which stars John Wayne*

BRING ON DE GOILS!

THE FILM was *Night After Night,* an otherwise unmemorable George Raft opus of the early 1930's. The scene was the entrance to a nightspot.

Enter Mae West, magnificently dripping in so much jewellery it must have given the lighting cameraman several heart attacks in his attempts to "damp it down" so that it didn't "flash up the bottle" as she moved.

Cries the hat-check girl: "Goodness! what lovely diamonds!"

Mae West: "Goodness . . . had nothing to do with it . . . dearie."

Gangsters' molls . . . they are part of the legend of the mobster movie. In *Night After Night* it was never openly established just what kind of a dame Mae West was playing, but with all those rocks she looked like the gangster's moll to top them all.

Let's stop the stutter of Chicago typewriters for a moment. Let's take a look at those gorgeous dames who shared bed and board with the screen hoodlums. They seemed to live out their lives in long, clinging, satin "negleejes".

They dangled cigarettes from sultry lips. They chewed gum and drank gin by the bath-tub load. Sometimes they got knocked about. Quite often they terrorized their menfolk; their ability to throw plates and hair-brushes often made a hoodlum's home look like a fairground coconut shy. In *The St. Valentine's Day Massacre* there is a battle-royal between Jean Hale, as the ex-chorine mistress, and George Segal, as Pete Gusenberg, which looks like openers for World War III.

Those gangsters' molls were rough, tough and ruthless. But what a great bunch of broads!

LEFT *One of the molls in* Portrait of a Mobster *(WB 1961)*
ABOVE *Part of the legend . . . the inimitable Mae West in* Night After Night *(Paramount 1932)*
OVERLEAF *Not all the gangster gals were molls, as is evident from this wedding picture in* The Godfather *(Alfan 1971)*

Joan Blondell

Friend of the heroine – good pal of the hero – wisecracking girl reporter – blowsy stud dealer . . . you name it, Joan Blondell has been right through the world of gangsterdom.

She originally came to Hollywood with James Cagney for *Sinner's Holiday* (1930), the film version of *Penny Arcade*, which both had played on Broadway. Then she was in *Public Enemy*, again with Cagney, and for several years she wandered through various Warner epics, including some second leads in musicals. For a time it looked as though Joan Blondell was destined to be always the second, never the first . . . until Tay Garnett cast her as the would-be starlet opposite Leslie Howard in *Stand-In* (1937). She stole the picture and made her name.

Nevertheless, Joan has never quite made it as the lead . . . and maybe she's better off that way. To watch her almost acting Edward G. Robinson off the screen as a fat, blowsy professional poker dealer in *The Cincinnati Kid* (1971) is an experience never to be forgotten.

Cyd Charisse

It's as a dancer that long-legged Cyd Charisse – she started life with the name of Tula Ellice Finkles, so who's to blame her for changing it? – usually gets mentioned in biographies. And certainly, as a dancer she should always be remembered with infinite pleasure, because in the late 1940's and early 1950's she made most of the so-called Hollywood female dancers look like Percherons hauling hay carts.

Nevertheless, she did get her chance to join the ranks of gangsters' molls. In *Party Girl* (1958) she played the part of a lady who was only as good as the Hays Office would allow her to show – today we'd probably call the character a call-girl and make no beautiful bones about it. But she was Lee J. Cobb's girl, and mobster Cobb did not like her paying attention to Robert Taylor, so he threatened to

BELOW *Joan Blondell played a professional poker dealer in* The Cincinnati Kid *(Filmways 1965)*
RIGHT *Tula Ellice Finkles . . . Cyd Charisse to you and me, in a scene from* Party Girl *(Eurtepe 1958)*

mark her face with acid.

It's rough on dames in that world of hoodlums. . . .

Mae Clarke

A musical comedy actress from Broadway – that was Mae Clarke. She was in *The Front Page* (1930) and the first version of *Waterloo Bridge* (1931).

But it is as the gangster's girl who got the grapefruit in her face from Jimmy Cagney (*Public Enemy* – 1931) that she earned her niche among the gangsters' girls.

Devotees of horror films may like to recall that Mae Clarke was there in the first *Frankenstein* (1931), swooning all over the place as the monster pursued her.

Glenda Farrell

Though girl reporters have never been like Glenda Farrell, there's no doubt they ought to have been. She made her picture debut in *Little Caesar* (1930) and from then on worked steadily in any number of crime movies.

Much of the time she was either friend of the heroine or wisecracking girl reporter. She supported Fay Wray through the terrors of *Mystery Of The Wax Museum* (1932) and eventually fled to the Torchy Blane series of B-pictures in which – surprise, surprise – she was a wisecracking girl reporter.

Gloria Grahame

If ever there was a gangster girl, it is Gloria Grahame, with her pouting mouth, her tiny voice, and her appearance of being there to be slapped as readily as she is to be loved.

Yet, strangely, her gangster-moll life is based on one performance only: as Lee Marvin's dame in *The Big Heat*, where she has scalding coffee thrown in her face and is thereafter disfigured. Hollywood coffee must be hotter than in any other town on the planet; you could get a cup of Soho coffee tossed in the kisser and feel nothing but a pleasant warmth, and in Montmartre you'd only be angry about the waste of a good drink.

Always, however, Gloria seems to have been the "other dame" in films; the day she gets her man and settles down to a dish-washer and babies . . . that'll be the day.

Gayle Hunnicutt

One doesn't expect Gayle Hunnicutt ever to have been anything but a lady. These days, she turns up in Hemdale pictures as somebody's wife – very

beautiful, but almost English.

Yet there was the time . . . in 1967 she was with Raymond Burr (yes, he could be nasty, despite *Ironside*) in *New Face In Hell* (in America: *P.J.*) and she played a . . . dare we say it . . . mistress. At the end of the film she gets her face blown off with a shot-gun, which seems to prove that being a mistress in a Hollywood thriller about a private eye is no way of ensuring a long life.

Carolyn Jones

A kook . . . that's the image which Carolyn Jones has projected on screen far too many times.

Far too many times, in fact, to let us remember that she was Mrs. Nelson in Don Siegel's film of *Baby Face Nelson* (1958). Tough on Mrs. Nelson: she wasn't Mrs. Nelson at all, but Mrs. Gillis, because "Baby Face" was christened Lester M. Gillis.

In the last big gun battle between "Baby Face" and the G-Men, two federal agents happened by chance to pass Nelson's coupe, in which were "Baby Face", Helen Gillis and one of his henchmen, John Paul Chase. Stupidly, "Baby Face" turned round and chased the federal men, who were killed in the resulting gunfight.

But "Baby Face" was killed, too . . . and Helen and Chase dumped his body in a ditch. It didn't help her: she was caught not long after and sent to prison.

That's what you get, Miss Carolyn Jones, for associating with Mickey Rooney . . .

Shirley MacLaine

In her long career in films, from *The Trouble With Harry* to her recent television series, long-legged Shirley MacLaine has been a true gangster's moll but once.

That single performance was enough to make her remembered when other broads are forgotten.

It was in *The Yellow Rolls-Royce*. With George C. Scott as her gangster lover, she was the personification of all the hoodlum dames that ever were. You knew she hit the gin bottle like liquor was going out of fashion. Without being told, you were sure she chewed gum in bed. You could be certain that when Mr. Scott was about his nefarious business, Shirley stayed home in the duplex apartment and played patience.

A great moll. She had what it takes – yessir, I'll tell the cockeyed world!

Barbara Nichols

Gangsters, it would seem, like their dames short,

cuddly and blonde . . . at least, in pictures. Barbara Nichols fulfils all three qualifications. A winner of several beauty contests while still at school – according to rumour, she was once "Miss Dill Pickle, U.S.A." which is a beautiful thought – she became a model and a chorus girl, then was whisked to Hollywood by a Warner executive.

Her true gangster-moll fame rests on two movies: *The George Raft Story*, in which she played the famous American night-club queen, Texas Guinan; and *The Scarface Mob*, where she was a stripper encumbered by the name of Brandy La France. Since then she seems to have devoted her talents – and, in the roles in which she specializes, she *has* talent – to television, and she can be seen on the box quite regularly.

Dorothy Provine

Bonnie Parker and Clyde Barrow were ambushed by federal agents at Shreveport, Louisiana on 23 May 1934 and shot to death. Of course, *Bonnie and Clyde* taught us that, didn't it?

What few people remember is that in 1958 there was a programme picture called *The Bonnie Parker Story* in which Dorothy Provine played Bonnie. (Hands up those who've seen it . . .)

It did not enshrine Miss Provine in the Chicago Hall of Fame, but it probably led to her television appearances in *The Roaring Twenties* series, where she was a hoofer in a Chicago night-club . . . and a very good comedy performance it was, too.

Lee Remick

This girl is an *actress*. In her early days, however, Lee Remick had her brushes with the criminal fraternity: in *Baby, The Rain Must Fall* (1965) she was married to Steve McQueen, a convict on parole, and before that, in *Experiment In Terror*, she suffered alongside Glenn Ford.

But good will triumph over evil . . . well, that's what they say. Lee Remick was married to policeman Frank Sinatra in *The Detective*, though there's no doubt that here she was a lady who just couldn't remain faithful to one man. Then, in that witty black comedy, *No Way To Treat A Lady*, she fell for detective George Segal, and that seems to prove that you can't keep a girl crooked forever.

One fascinating item of information: at 12 years old, with her school drama society, she played Mrs de Winter in a production of *Rebecca*. That dramatic society knew its casting.

Lizabeth Scott

In the 1950's, Lizabeth Scott always seemed to be

TOP LEFT *That famous coffee-in-the-face scene from* The Big Heat *(Columbia 1953). Gloria Grahame gets first aid, Lee Marvin holds the coffee pot*
TOP RIGHT *What a dame! Shirley MacLaine with George C. Scott in* The Yellow Rolls Royce *(MGM 1964)*
ABOVE LEFT *Mickey Rooney is supported on his last few yards by Carolyn Jones, in* Baby Face Nelson *(Fryman-Zimbalist 1957)*
ABOVE RIGHT *They don't come any tougher. Dorothy Provine in* The Bonnie Parker Story *(AIP 1956)*

ABOVE *Shelley Winters is likeable, no matter how nasty she turns in* Bloody Mama *(AIP 1969)*
RIGHT *Raquel Welch and Frank Sinatra in* Lady in Cement *(Arcola-Millfield 1968)*

moving through films in parts where she didn't have to do much except lean against doorways and play sultry. Usually she was somebody's girl friend . . . yes, they called 'em girl friends in those days . . . and it was painfully obvious that her relationship with Wendell Corey or Edmund O'Brien or Robert Ryan was not one on which polite society would confer a smile.

But . . . and this is important . . . Lizabeth Scott had her minor triumph in *Pulp*, that parody of the private-eye thriller which almost came off. She played the *femme fatale* of the story, and almost succeeded in upstaging Mickey Rooney, one of the most difficult tasks in movies.

A talented lady, Lizabeth Scott is notable for a deep, dark, apparently-gin-soaked voice. That is probably why her first acting job was as understudy to Tallulah Bankhead.

Fay Spain

Mrs. Capone – that is Fay Spain's *niche* in the hierarchy of film gangsterdom. In *Al Capone* she married Rod Steiger and wallowed in domesticity.

In fact, she was not a moll at all, but a highly respectable housewife who stayed well out of the shooting. This was certainly true to life; Mae Capone remained well out of the limelight and even resisted having her picture taken.

Shelley Winters

It's difficult to believe in Shelley Winters being nasty. That is why, when she played Ma Barker in *Bloody Mama* (1970) the audience's sympathy was with her most of the way, no matter how repulsive she tried to be.

Bad luck, Miss Winters. You're destined to be the jolly gangster lady, the one with the sharp tongue and the ready wit, and sometimes underneath it all, the heart of gold. You are more likely to be believed as Polly in *A House Is Not A Home* than as a virago with a tommy-gun.

Nevertheless, Miss Winters has had a long association with criminals on screen. She was with Barry Sullivan in *The Gangster* (1947) and she played in *Johnny Stool Pigeon* (1949). When *High Sierra* was remade as *I Died A Thousand Times* (1955), she was in there pitching with Jack Palance and Lee Marvin. She even turned up in *The Moving Target,* opposite Paul Newman. You cannot, it seems, keep a good gun-moll down.

McGurk, the New York private eye played by Burt Reynolds in Shamus *(Columbia/Westman 1972) is kept busy throughout (left, right and below right). The movie also starred Dyan Cannon*
BELOW *The Burglars (Columbia Films/Video 1971) starred Omar Sharif and Jean-Paul Belmondo*

MURDER COMES EASY

IN MOVIE gangland, death is usually but the drop of a gun away. It's fictionalized and stylized and only the baddies die violently. But it is sudden death.

Because the gangster is closely associated with the gun, most of the killings in film mobsterland have been done with bullets. Film gangsters don't die in peace . . . though the exception was Marlon Brando as *The Godfather,* collapsing with a heart attack among his tomato plants. Film gangsters don't get poisoned, nor do they die of old age. They tend to get shot to death in a hail of bullets . . . usually lasting much longer than the magazine of a tommy-gun.

In the *St. Valentine's Day Massacre,* the gang-sters met their end in a small garage at 2122 North Clark Street, Chicago. Seven Members of George "Bugs" Moran's gang were slain shortly after 11 o'clock on the morning of 14 February 1929. Two men dressed in police uniforms, accompanied by two fake plain-clothes officers, entered the garage, fired 140 bullets from two tommy-guns and mowed down the opposition.

St. Valentine's Day, 1929, marked the culmina-tion of the great Chicago gang wars. Though the gangsters did not appreciate it, from that moment on, they were on their way.

Nevertheless, gangland continued to kill, and be killed. In *The Finger Points,* Richard Barthelmess was put on the spot as a crooked reporter. The kill-ing was based on the story of Jake Lingle, police reporter for the *Chicago Tribune,* who was once described as the "unofficial chief of police of Chicago." His weekly pay from the newspaper was $65: at the time of his death he had $60,000 in his personal account . . . and he owned a diamond-studded belt, the gift of Al Capone. Who ordered the death of Jake Lingle in the crowded subway at Michigan Boulevard has never officially been proved, but the snub-nosed .38 with which he was shot was bought by two "Bugs" Moran gunmen who changed sides to join with Capone.

Getting rid of the opposition sometimes called for a considerable degree of ingenuity in motion picture gangland. In *Murder Incorporated,* the stool-pigeon whom the "Syndicate" needs to eliminate – in order to prevent him giving evidence – is thrown from a high window.

FAR LEFT Magnum Force *(Malpaso 1973) owes its title to the gun which Clint Eastwood carries*
LEFT *Film gangsters don't die in peace. A disfigured Gloria Grahame makes sure that Lee Marvin gets the message from a snub-nosed police special in* The Big Heat *(Columbia 1953)*

133

ABOVE *Alain Delon (with gun right) and Jean-Paul Belmondo (with gun left) come together in* Borsalino *(Adel/Marianne/Mars 1970)*
RIGHT *Though Marlon Brando died relatively peacefully in* The Godfather *(Alfan 1971), a lot of guys didn't*

Even better – in terms of ingenuity – was the action of Eli Wallach in *The Lineup*. This was a film about heroin smuggling; in it, Eli Wallach as a psychopath dope runner, gets rid of his boss – a man confined to a wheelchair – by pushing him from a balcony to the floor of an ice-rink.

Lee Marvin is a hoodlum with the ability to rid himself of the opposition in a variety of ways. Though he normally employs a gun, he is not above contemptuously tossing a rival mobster over the balcony of his apartment, as in *Point Blank*.

Your professional contractor, the man who is employed by gangsters to knock off someone he does not even know, works out methods of murder that do not involve him. *Murder By Contract,* an otherwise unremarkable film, portrays this admirably. In one sequence Vince Edwards, as the hired hit man, plots a way of murdering a witness by causing her to be electrocuted when she switches on the TV. That it doesn't work because she has a remote control radio-switch for her television is the beginning of the contractor's downfall.

In *The Mechanic,* Charles Bronson is a hit man who plans his murders with the care of Montgomery going up against Rommel in World War II. His idea of a good clean kill is when the victim is blown to pieces without even knowing he was on the spot.

Usually, however, it comes back to guns. These days, a really reliable contractor is more likely to be hired by a terrorist organization than by gangsters. Such a man is Edward Fox in *Day Of The Jackal,* a cool, impersonal killer who spends weeks setting up the contract, has his rifle specially-made, and lets nobody and nothing stand in his way as he slowly but surely moves to the attempted assassination of President de Gaulle. It didn't happen? Don't be too sure about that. The film makes it seem likely that it could have happened . . . up to the final second.

Making murder come easy is part of the build-up of the gangster film, and not until *Bonnie and Clyde* was it shown that bullets bite deep . . . and bring blood.

The end of Cagney in *White Heat* (1949) is akin to this old-style method of showing the death, but none of the pain. It is the last reel, the plan to rob a chemical plant's pay office has failed, and Cagney – as the leader of the gang – is cornered on top of a huge gas tank. "Top of the world, ma!" he screams, as he empties his gun at the police . . . who obligingly reply in kind, blowing up Cagney, tank and all. It looks good on screen, but a moment's thought suggests that this could not have been a pleasant way to go.

The bizarre kill, as opposed to the straightforward "Let-him-have-it-Mac" method, is well demonstrated in *Bloody Mama,* Roger Corman's film about Ma Barker. There's a moment when a friendly girl swimmer meets up with "Doc" Barker. He talks her into going back to the gang's shack, ties her to the bed, rapes her . . . and then the gang, with Ma Barker leading, take considerable care in drowning her in the bath-tub.

It only goes to show that you shouldn't chat up your local neighbourhood gangster . . .

LEFT *"Most of the killings in movie mobsterland are done with bullets."* If Rod
Steiger, in Al Capone *(Burrows-Ackerman-Allied Artists 1958)* doesn't stop,
he'll add strangling to the list
ABOVE *A scene from the 1960 production of* Murder Inc. *(Princess Prod.
Corp./20th Century-Fox)*
BELOW *Moment of fear for the traitor. Zero Mostel knows he's for it in the
1951 production of* Murder Inc. *(United States Pictures). In the States this
movie was called* The Enforcer

The end of Omar Sharif (above) *and another hood* (left) *in* The Burglars *(Columbia Films/Video 1971). The mark over the man's left eye is a bullet hole*

ABOVE RIGHT *One move and you get it. Charles Bronson up against a knife in* The Valachi Papers *(De Laurentiis 1972)*

RIGHT *Jean-Paul Belmondo in another athletic scene from* The Burglars

TOP *Steve McQueen notches up another baddie in* The Getaway *(Astral/ Foster-Brower 1972)*
ABOVE *Cagney exits in the arms of Gladys George in* The Roaring Twenties *(Warners 1939)*
RIGHT *Vince Edwards works out another way of getting rid of Billie Williams in* Murder by Contract *(Orbit 1958)*

Odd Men Out

A gangster is always a criminal. But a criminal is not necessarily a gangster.

The dictionary defines a gangster as: a hooligan, a hardened criminal. If this were true, every experienced peterman with a record of a dozen or so blown safes could be described as a gangster. He might be, but it is much more likely that he is a criminal on his own, either doing a job for personal gain or hired by an organization to blow the safe on their behalf.

The leader of that organization – the man – Mr Big – the big fellow – the boss . . . he is the gangster. He is also very much an American phenomenon. Though it is not strictly true to say that he was born of Prohibition, it is a fact that Prohibition – "a swell law to break, the very best one on the book", as a Chicago newspaper man wrote in 1930 – brought the gangster forcefully into the public eye.

As far as movies were concerned, gangsters stayed strictly Hollywood for a long time. Britain had its crook melodramas, but they were mainly concerned with drawing-room detectives, very often films adapted from successful stage thrillers. Typical of that era was *The Crooked Billet*, with a young Madeleine Carroll looking beautiful and helpless in a story about missing jewels set in a country inn which gave the film its title. For a long time, the gangster in a British crime picture appeared to live above a night club somewhere off Greek Street, in which the floor show consisted of a tired blonde in a long satin evening dress; the gangster himself was invariably suave, with a pencil-line moustache, pointed shoes and a tightly-buttoned double-breasted jacket with wide stripes. There was, in fact, a British film of the 1930's called *Greek Street,* in which the luscious Sari Maritza appeared, and the villain looked like that.

Across the North Sea, in Germany, the state-aided cinema industry invented its own super-gangster in *Dr Mabuse* (1922). A two-part film, produced by Erich Pommer and directed by Fritz Lang, it appeared under the generic title of *Dr Mabus Der Spieler;* Part 1 – *Dr Mabuse Der Spieler – Ein Bild Der Zeit:* Part 2 – *Inferno – Menschen Der Seit.*

Dr Mabuse, however, is not a gangster in the Chicago fashion. He is a super-crook controlling a vast empire of crime which seems to rob banks and fight law and order more with the intention of destroying Germanic civilization than of making a dishonest mark. In that respect, he is more akin to the infamous Dr Fu-Manchu than he is to Al Capone.

Among the early gangster films of Europe must be included *Pépé Le Moko* (1937), with that solid rock of French films, Jean Gabin. Remade as *Algiers* by Hollywood a year later with Hedy Lamarr and Charles Boyer, it was not shown again until after World War II, when a comparison could be made between the original French film and the American version. The French film, as was the way of French movies in the 1930's, is almost painfully slow; though *Algiers* is not likely to win critical awards, it does have the merit of pace and excitement.

Not until after World War II, did the European gangster begin to show his teeth . . . and his guns. *No Orchids For Miss Blandish* was a painfully inept British version of the James Hadley Chase gangster thriller, with Jack La Rue snarling wickedly at all the right moments. A better British gangster film was *Noose* (1948), in which Nigel Patrick gave an excellent performance as a post-war spiv, involved in everything from black market deals to theft.

France produced the best European gangster film of the post-war years with *Du Rififi Chez Les Hommes* (1955) (retitled: *Rififi Means Trouble* in the English version). Directed by Jules Dassin – an American, despite the name – who had already made very good hoodlum movies like *Brute Force* and *The Naked City* in Hollywood, *Rififi* featured Jean Serrais, Carl Molnier and Dassin himself and contains most of the elements of the true gangster thriller: the bringing together of the gang, the planning of the jewel robbery, the robbery itself (a 20-minute sequence without a whisper on the sound track), and the quarrel towards the end. There is even the inevitable squealer, rubbed out for his treachery, and an exciting auto-chase sequence.

Touchez Pas Au Grisbi, a film of Jacques Becker, was made a year earlier than *Rififi* and starred Jean Gabin, without whom no French gangster film seems quite complete. It is not very well known in either Britain or America; in fact, it gained a London release after *Rififi* had made such a success in Britain. Yet it is an extremely exciting gangster

ABOVE RIGHT *The German super-gangster, Dr Mabuse controlled a vast empire of crime, scene from* Dr Mabuse der Spieler *(Atlas 1922)*
RIGHT *Jack La Rue and Linden Travers in* No Orchids for Miss Blandish *(Renown 1948)*

Dr. Mabuse
der Spieler

ein Atlas Film

ABOVE *Alain Delon played a hired killer in* Le Samourai *(Filmel/C.I.C.C. (Paris)/Fida Cinematografica (Rome) 1967), but in this scene he is at the wrong end of a gun held by Jacques Leroy*

BELOW Pepe Le Moko *was remade in Hollywood as* Algiers *(Wanger 1938). From left to right are Joseph Calleia, Charles Boyer and Sigrid Gurie*

RIGHT *In* Alphaville *(Chaumiane 1965) Eddy Constantine was Lemmy Caution*

movie, with a gold robbery, a battle between rival gangs and a shoot-out climax on a country road, with bombs exploding and machine-guns blazing.

The success of these two films sparked off something of a vogue for gangster films in the French cinema of the 1950's and 1960's. The *Rififi* symbol was exploited further with *Rififi a Tokyo*, made by MGM in 1962 and starring Charles Vanel; little is ever heard of this, in common with *Du Rififi a Paname* (titled in English: *Rififi In Paris* . . . which sounds rather odd), in which Jean Gabin appeared.

All three of France's movie gangsters turned up in *Le Clan Des Siciliens* (1969); Jean Gabin, Alain Delon and Jean-Paul Belmondo, along with that much neglected American actor, Sydney Chaplin. This was the story of a robbery aboard a plane, before airline hi-jacks became a commonplace.

Delon, of course, had already made something of a name for himself two years earlier, when *Le Samourai* showed him as a hired killer, poker-faced, ruthless – very much the sort of character which Alan Ladd made his own in *This Gun For Hire*.

Belmondo had followed a similar road, often playing roles with a suggestion of James Bond in them. *L'Homme De Rio* (1963) is a case in point; as some kind of a secret agent he risks life and limb throughout the entire film . . . but always with a smile. More recently, he showed almost the gaiety and athletic expertise of a modern Fairbanks in *The Burglars*, particularly in the sequence – made without doubles – in which he jumps from buses to cars and back again while being chased by Omar Sharif. It could be that Belmondo's grace of movement stems from the fact that he is descended from Fanny Cerrito, a famous ballet-dancer of the 19th century.

Delon and Belmondo came together again with considerable success in 1970, when they made *Borsalino*. An affectionate glance at the old-style gangster film translated to a Marseilles setting, at times it looks a bit of a spoof. It is, however, immensely exciting and though it never seemed to gain a major release in the English-speaking world, it is worth tracking down.

One interesting phenomenon produced by the French gangster cinema of the 1950's was Lemmy Caution.

Mr Caution, fast-talking, hard-drinking, tough as a chrome-steel spanner, was an F.B.I. agent created by a British writer called Peter Cheyney. Strangely enough, Cheyney, who flourished during the 1940's, is largely ignored as a serious crime-

fiction author today, yet at the time his Lemmy Caution novels – as un-American as Dashiel Hammett trying to write a story about the Suffolk countryside – had a tremendous following.

Better than the Lemmy Caution stories, in fact, are Cheyney's private-eye novels about Slim Callaghan, carefully patterned on the Philip Marlowe image but set in London; and also his excellent spy thrillers of World War II. Callaghan was played once on screen in a British film called *Uneasy Terms* (1948), with Michael Rennie as the detective. But it was Lemmy Caution who caught the attention of the French cinema, and as Lemmy, an American singer called Eddie Constantine.

Only one of his Lemmy Caution adventures seems to have survived into the 1970's: *Alphaville, A Strange Adventure of Lemmy Caution* (1965). Directed by Jean-Luc Godard, it bore about as much resemblance to the adventures of an F.B.I. agent as *Tarzan* must have done to a documentary about Africa. It wasn't supposed to; this was a fantasy about the comic-strip hero, and Godard merely used Lemmy Caution as a symbol.

ABOVE *Stanley Baker is a British actor who can really get tough. Here he is in*
The Criminal *(Merton Park 1960)*
RIGHT *Michael Caine forces Geraldine Moffatt into the trunk of a car in*
Get Carter *(MGM 1971)*

Meanwhile, in the 1950's, the British gangster film was languishing. Dassin was brought to London to make *Night And The City* with Richard Widmark. It was a heavily symbolic piece of movie gangsterism, with Francis L. Sullivan suave and sinister as the villain, and Widmark spending most of the film on the run from his enemies. Herbert Lom was a big-time mobster, and looked decidedly uncomfortable about the whole thing.

In 1954, Laurence Harvey led a London gang in *The Good Die Young,* with Gloria Grahame as the girl. It didn't ring true; despite the introduction of Stanley Baker, on his way to becoming the best British tough guy of them all, it was difficult to believe that the character played by Harvey would have the strength to weld a gang together. Baker went from strength to strength in tough roles, as an old lag in *The Criminal* (1961) and a policeman in *Blind Date* (1960) and *The Offence* (1972).

The best example of British gangsterdom, without a doubt, is also the most recent: *Get Carter* (1971) with Michael Caine.

This is a gangster movie which takes the central figure – hardly the hero, because Carter is an acknowledged baddie – out of the confines of Soho and away up north to the gangland of Newcastle-upon-Tyne. The plot concerns Carter's efforts to

discover who was responsible for the death of his brother; against the wishes of his London gang-boss he takes the train to Newcastle (reading a Raymond Chandler novel on the way) and embarks upon a single-handed crusade of violence against the north-country gangsters.

It is a film which, in its way, is as ruthless as *Dirty Harry*. Carter locks a girl witness – not a particularly pleasant young woman, but that's beside the point – in the trunk of a car. When the car is pushed into the Tyne and the girl is drowned, he betrays no emotion. He shoots a dope-addict woman full of too much heroin and leaves her to die. At the finish he is shot by an emissary of his own people, much as crooked detective Quinn is killed in *Across 110th Street*. We do not feel anything. Carter was a crook and a murderer; he just happened to be a crook and a murderer pursuing his own private vendetta.

But it's an exciting film for all that. It raises some hope for the future of the British gangster film, showing London mobsters for what they really are: ruthless, brutal and cruel. If *Public Enemy* was created out of Al Capone and Hymie Weiss, it seems more than likely that *Get Carter* had its origins in the Kray Brothers and the Richardson gang.

146

ABOVE Borsalino *(Adel/Marianne/Mars 1970) is an affectionate glance at the old-style gangster film translated to a Marseilles setting. Alain Delon (left) and Jean-Paul Belmondo (right) behind the wheel of a Lorraine-Dietrich* RIGHT *In* Magnum Force *(Malpaso 1973) Clint Eastwood has few friends*

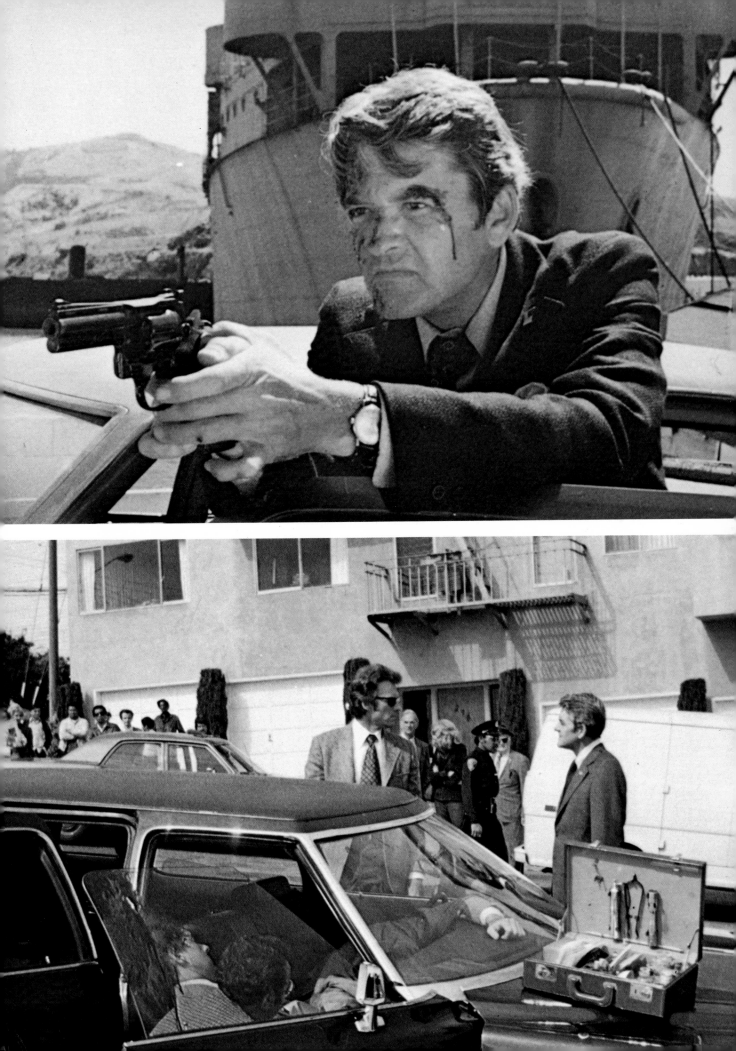

In 99 and 44/100% Dead *(20th Century-Fox 1974) two rival gangs struggle for power. Richard Harris (above) is a hired professional killer and Chuck Connors, with the "claw" is his main adversary*

THE MOST outworn *cliché* about crime is that it does not pay. In fact, the rewards of crime can become very high indeed – as long as one is prepared to accept the associated risk of being caught.

On screen, crime certainly pays very handsomely, as *The Godfather* proved for Paramount. Gangsters are big business in the criminal world, and they are also big business at the box office.

But . . . do they have a future?

As long as there are criminals, films will be made about their exploits. Though what we call "a gangster film" in the 1970's bears little resemblance to the classics of the 1930's, it is still a film about big-time criminals and organized crime. Only the baddies have been changed to assist identification.

Badge 373 (1973) is a case in point. It is a simple story, based on the exploits of Eddie Egan, a real New York policeman who also, for good measure, plays a part in the film. Ryan, a New York detective, is suspended for causing the death of a Puerto Rican dope runner. Taking a job as a bartender, he learns that his old partner on the force has been killed. Then, with the law against him because he is no longer a policeman, and harassed also by the villains, he sets out to avenge his friend's murder.

The twist is that these villains are no longer bootleggers, heroin smugglers, big-time gamblers or bank robbers. They are Puerto Ricans. Some of them are men who seek to foment a revolution on their island; others, led by a sinister figure in dark glasses called Sweet William, are the crooked element who will supply the necessary guns and ammunition. Ryan, played by Robert Duvall, wages his own solitary war against both parties.

It's a rough, tough and ruthless film, in which Duvall is as brutal as his adversaries; towards the end, he callously chops down a night watchman in order to gain entrance to the Brooklyn docks. In fact, it is very difficult to have sympathy for any of the characters in *Badge 373*. Perhaps this is intentional. Perhaps cinema audiences of the future will not require to identify sympathetically with the characters they watch.

Certainly, this was true in *The French Connection*. No one could deny that it is a tremendously exciting film . . . but could anyone have a feeling of sympathetic identification with the central cop character? Gene Hackman stirred the blood, but it was difficult to be concerned about whether he lived or died.

Villains, then are changing . . . and so are the heroes, if they can still be described by a word which means: "an illustrious warrior: one greatly regarded for his achievements or qualities."

The gangster film of the future will be tougher than its predecessors. The characters in it will be more brutal. The blood will be bloodier. The killings will be done with more ruthlessness . . . and, one fears, greater attention to gory detail.

A pity, perhaps, but the present-day screen seems determined to mirror life in almost documentary detail. Criminal life is violent, so gangster movies portray violence red and raw.

Many years ago, in a film called *To Mary, With Love*, Myrna Loy uttered a classic line. In that plaintive, slightly cracking voice she commented: "People are always saying. *Why can't the movies be more like life?* I say, *Why can't life be more like the movies?*"

It's a line which today has little application to the screen as a whole. As far as the gangster film is concerned, it is totally out of date.

The Godfather showed that organized crime pays very well indeed. It also demonstrated that big-time gangsters are utterly ruthless – indeed, have to be ruthless in order to remain at the top. The last scenes of *The Godfather*, as enemy after enemy is mown down while Al Pacino, as the new head of the gang, attends a christening, are a study in calculated screen violence.

The wisdom or otherwise of this cinema pattern need not be debated here. It does seem unlikely,

ABOVE LEFT *There's plenty of excitement in* 99 and 44/100% Dead *(20th Century-Fox 1974)*
LEFT *In* Shaft *(MGM 1971) Richard Rowntree is not only articulate, but also tough*

however, that the violent screen of gangsterdom will ever return to those days of innocence when Cagney, riddled with bullets, could die at his mother's feet with never a speck of blood about him.

What about the villains? Gangster films seldom bother to show in clinical detail how the baddies flourish down there in the underworld. Once they were bootleggers, and it was accepted that this was a criminal undertaking which should be demolished. Or they were involved in "the numbers racket" or "the protection racket" or "the dope racket" or whatever seemed fashionable at the time.

The coming villains are likely to be connected with the Mafia. Not long ago the Mafia was lumped in films along with the Syndicate, the Organization, or sometimes just the Mob.

That the United States has a nationwide underworld which feeds information from state to state, handles extortion and robbery on a vast scale, and often operates behind a facade of respectable business enterprises, is a fact. That it is quite as tightly-knit an organization as films like *Murder Incorporated* and *The Valachi Papers* tend to imply, is a matter of speculation.

The Brotherhood (1968), is a film about the Mafia which has been strangely neglected. The story of a *mafioso* (Kirk Douglas) and his battle for power, it received some adverse comments at the time of its release because it showed a scene in which two men kissed. The critics could not have realized that this was the Mafia "kiss of death"; since then, audiences have become more knowledgeable about the ways of *Cosa Nostra*.

Shaft pointed the way towards films in which the hero could be not only a tough private eye, but also a black eye, too. Since then there have been *Shaft's Big Score*, and *Shaft in Africa*. One feels that this might continue to the point where we have *Shaft Meets The Black Wolfman*, but it is to be hoped that the cycle will have run its course before then.

Nevertheless, black heroes – and black villains, too – are nowadays flourishing like the green bay tree. *Slaughter* gave us ex-football player Jim Brown roaring through the underworld to avenge the death of his parents; exactly why they were murdered by the underworld in the first place seemed a little obscure, but it was not essential to the action, and *Slaughter* was first and foremost a film in which action replaced characterization and plot.

Black heroes become involved with the murders

of white gangsters pushing drugs for the Mafia in *Come Back Charleston Blue* (1973). There are also echoes of the Dutch Schultz days, for the gangsters are killed by having their throats cut by razors identified as belonging to Charleston Blue, a black gangster slain by Schultz in 1932. Top that for combining all the elements if you can.

Come Back Charleston Blue is based on the novel, *The Heat's On,* by Chester Himes, creator of those two black police detectives, Gravedigger Jones and Coffin Ed (Godfrey Cambridge and Raymond St. Jacques). It leans strongly towards comedy, both in construction and in the playing of the two detectives, who have a casual approach to their job which contrasts well with the average white screen cop.

This suggestion that not all black men on screen are as lily-white – or should it be black? – as the Sydney Poitier type of screen character is also excellently demonstrated in *Trick Baby* (1973), a film which seemed to slip by the critics.

The story is that of two con-men: White Folks (Kiel Martin), who had a black mother and a white father and whose skin is white; and Blue Howard (Mel Stewart), a grizzled black veteran who has taught the younger man everything he knows about the art of the confidence trickster. Together they dupe the Mafia and the police; they make $10,000 and have to give some of it away to the local black protection merchant; they set up a confidence property deal to swindle some over-greedy white businessmen out of $150,000, but cannot quite get hold of the loot; and eventually Blue is shot to death by white gunmen on the pay-roll of a Mafia (yes, the Mafia's right there again) leader, because it was his uncle they conned out of $10,000 at the beginning of the picture.

The quality of *Trick Baby* is that not all the blacks are all good, and not all the whites are all bad. What is more, it makes a point of showing that black men can play on their colour to gain their own ends.

The new crop of gangster films almost tends to verge on parody, though the movies remain just as exciting and perhaps even bloodier than before. Clint Eastwood has followed *Dirty Harry* with *Magnum Force,* a title which obviously capitalizes on the impact made by his use of the Magnum .44 hand-gun in the earlier picture. Once again he is a ruthless city cop battling against the forces of evil; if anything, he is even tougher than in the previous movie.

Then comes *99 And 44/100% Dead,* the John Frankenheimer film for 20th-Century-Fox. (The title, incidentally, is a play on an old advertisement

ABOVE *It may look odd, but the kiss of death is how the Mafia is said to put the finger on someone it wants out of the way: Charles Bronson in a scene from* The Valachi Papers *(De Laurentiis 1972)*
OVERLEAF *Al Pacino and Marlon Brando in* The Godfather *(Alfan 1971)*

for an American brand of soap, which was always sloganned as "99 and 44/100% pure.") Basically, it is the age-old theme of a struggle for power between two rival gangs, one led by Uncle Frank (Edmond O'Brien) and the other by Big Eddie (Bradford Dillman). Uncle Frank hires professional killer Harry Crown (Richard Harris), while Big Eddie sends for Marvin "Claw" Zuckerman (Chuck Connors). People get shot, dynamited, beaten up and blown sky-high. There's a whole bordello full of beautiful girls called "Dolly's Incorporated" and plenty of fighting between Harris and Connors.

The mixture as before? Well, yes, except that Frankenheimer has tended to film this as a satire on gangsterdom.

The gangster film has changed, because gangsters themselves have changed. Al Capone is long dead. *The Godfather* and Sweet William have taken his place. The Mustang and the Thunderbird have replaced the Chevvy sedan. The machine-carbine's staccato rattle has taken over from the thudding roar of a drum-magazine Thompson. Edward G. Robinson has gone and Cagney has retired to Martha's Vineyard to write his memoirs.

But the gangster film will continue. "Get this, pal – it'll kill you." It sure will.

Acknowledgments

The publishers owe a debt of gratitude to the numerous people who have helped make this book possible by allowing them the run of their collections of stills and memorabilia and by putting information of one kind or another at their disposal.

The publishers are particularly grateful to the Alan Frank Collection for the provision of stills and invaluable information; to the staff of all departments of the British Film Institute; to Cinema International Corp (UK), Paramount, MGM, Columbia-Warners and Scotia Barber Associates; to Twentieth Century-Fox for stills from *99 and 44/100% Dead*, *The St. Valentine's Day Massacre*, *Murder Inc.*, *Roger Touhy – Gangster*, *The Salzburg Connection*, *The French Connection* and *Lady in Cement*.

Finally to all those in the film industry without whom this book would have been impossible goes a special thankyou.

INDEX OF FILM TITLES

GENERAL INDEX

First published 1974 by Octopus Books Limited, 59 Grosvenor Street, London W1

ISBN 0 7064 0370 3

© 1974 Octopus Books Limited

Produced by Mandarin Publishers Limited, 14 Westlands Road, Quarry Bay, Hong Kong

Printed in Hong Kong